Some Surprises from the Apostle Paul

Some Surprises from the Apostle Paul

William O. Walker, Jr.

POLEBRIDGE PRESS
Salem, Oregon

Polebridge Press is the publishing arm of the Westar Institute, a non-profit, public-benefit research and educational organization. To learn more, visit westarinstitute.org.

Cover and interior design by Robaire Ream

Library of Congress Cataloging-in-Publication Data
Names: Walker, William O., Jr., 1930- author.
Title: Some surprises from the Apostle Paul / by William O. Walker, Jr.
Description: Salem, OR : Polebridge Press, 2017. | Includes bibliographical
    references and index.
Identifiers: LCCN 2016033120 | ISBN 9781598151800 (alk. paper)
Subjects: LCSH: Bible. Epistles of Paul--Criticism, interpretation, etc. |
    Paul, the Apostle, Saint.
Classification: LCC BS2650.52 .W355 2017 | DDC 227/.06--dc23
LC record available at https://lccn.loc.gov/2016033120
10   9   8   7   6   5   4   3   2   1

Contents

Acknowledgments

I have been studying the letters of Paul for more than half a century and have published many of my findings in two books: *Interpolations in the Pauline Letters*, published by Sheffield Academic Press in 2001, and *Paul and His Legacy: Collected Essays*, published by Polebridge Press in 2015. These books were intended for scholars in the field of New Testament Studies. The present volume, however, is intended for a broader audience, including pastors, Christian educators, interested laypeople, and the general public. For the most part, the volume is based on a series of lectures I delivered some years ago, first at the SoL (Source of Light) Center at University Presbyterian Church in San Antonio, Texas, and later at Madison Square Presbyterian Church, also in San Antonio, and several articles that I have published in recent years in *The Fourth R: An Advocate for Religious Literacy*. Because most of the material in the book was originally delivered as public lectures, I have retained the somewhat informal style of the lectures. For the same reason, there is some repetition in the various chapters

I am grateful to Larry Alexander, formerly publisher of Polebridge Press, for accepting my proposal to publish this volume, and, as always, I cannot praise highly enough the Polebridge Press team of Cassandra Farrin, Barbara Hampson, Char Matejovsky, and Robaire Ream. They are true professionals, and it is a joy to work with them!

My thanks to Robert J. Miller, editor, for permission to include revised versions of articles published in *The Fourth R* as chapters 3, 6, 7, 8, and 9 in this volume. My thanks, also, to Bloomsbury Publishing Plc for permission to include in chapter 9 material from my book, *Interpolations in the Pauline Letters*.

I am pleased to dedicate this book to the members of Madison Square Presbyterian Church—not only because some of them were present and responded favorably when I presented these materials in the Sunday morning adult class but also because, for more than fifteen years, they have "welcomed me home" as a part of their community.

Abbreviations

Col	Colossians
1, 2 Cor	1, 2 Corinthians
Eph	Ephesians
Gal	Galatians
Gen	Genesis
Isa	Isaiah
Jas	James
Matt	Matthew
1, 2 Pet	1, 2 Peter
Phlm	Philemon
Phil	Philippians
Ps	Psalm
Rev	Revelation
Rom	Romans
1, 2 Thess	1, 2 Thessalonians
1, 2 Tim	1, 2 Timothy

Preface

It is no exaggeration to say that the Apostle Paul dominates the New Testament. Thirteen of its twenty-seven books claim him as their author;* roughly two-thirds of another (Acts of the Apostles) has him as its main character; still another (2 Peter) briefly mentions him by name; and a compelling argument can be made that two others (James and Matthew) have Paul, his letters, and/or Pauline Christianity in mind in some of what they say.[1] Thus, it is not surprising that Paul has often been characterized as "the first Christian theologian." Indeed, contemporary German New Testament scholar Gerd Lüdemann not only refers to him as "the most important figure in primitive Christianity and in the Church until today" but also labels him "the Founder of Christianity."[2]

Although my own judgment is that these latter characterizations are hyperbolic at best and misleading at worst, it cannot be denied that Paul played a critically important role in the development and spread of what came to be known as "Christianity." Moreover, his letters profoundly influenced the thought of such major Christian theologians as St. Augustine (354–430), Martin Luther (1483–1546), and Karl Barth (1886–1968); they played a key role in the Protestant Reformation; and they continue to form the basis for much of what we know today as Christian theology. Thus, I think Lüdemann is correct in insisting "that

---

*As will be noted in the Introduction, however, six of these books—1 Timothy, 2 Timothy, Titus, Ephesians, Colossians, and 2 Thessalonians—are likely "pseudonymous" (that is, written not by Paul but by other authors using Paul's name). Only 1 Thessalonians, 1 Corinthians, 2 Corinthians, Galatians, Philippians, Philemon, and Romans are generally regarded as authentically Pauline. As will also be noted in the Introduction, however, even these books, with the exception of Philemon, have almost certainly been edited, revised, and/or augmented in various ways.

both Christians and non-Christians must come to terms with Paul, in order to be able to redefine their place within or outside Christianity in the light of any new insights into the apostle's life and thought."[3]

Our knowledge about Paul comes almost exclusively from his own letters, which were composed approximately twenty to thirty years after the death of Jesus (c. 50–60 CE) and thus are almost certainly the earliest surviving Christian writings. Although the book of Acts purports to provide considerable information regarding Paul and his activities, it was likely written more than half a century after the lifetime of Paul,[4] and we have no idea what source or sources the author may have used. Indeed, much of the material appears to be simply extrapolations from what Paul himself wrote in his letters, modified and amplified to suit the theological and apologetic agendas of the author.[5] Later Christian writings purport to provide additional information regarding Paul,[6] but, as in the case of Acts, such information is of doubtful historical value; indeed, most of it is clearly legendary. Thus, it is to Paul's letters that we must look if we wish to understand the apostle and his thought.

Roughly speaking, Paul was a contemporary of Jesus. Although he apparently was living in Jerusalem at the time of Jesus' presence there, he almost certainly did not know Jesus during the latter's lifetime. Initially, Paul was a zealous Jew who, in his own words, "was violently persecuting the church of God and trying to destroy it" (Gal 1:13). Something happened, though, that transformed him into an equally zealous proclaimer of the faith he had attempted to destroy. In his letters, he speaks of this "something" only in rather cryptic terms: "Have I not seen the Lord?" (1 Cor 9:1), Christ "appeared to me" (1 Cor 15:8), and God "was pleased to reveal his Son to me" (Gal 1:15–16).[7] During the two to three decades following this experience, Paul traveled extensively in Syria, Asia Minor, and Greece (known as Macedonia and Achaia in New Testament times) proclaiming the gospel of Christ and establishing churches. In his letter to the Romans, which may be his latest surviving letter, he indicates his intention to go to Rome and then, hopefully, to Spain. Although the evidence is hazy, he almost certainly was arrested, imprisoned, and eventually executed in

Rome sometime in the early 60s CE (perhaps during the emperor Nero's "persecution" of Christians in 64 CE). Despite legends to the contrary, it is doubtful that Paul ever went to Spain.

Paul has always been a controversial figure. His own letters make it clear that this was true during his lifetime. In 1 Corinthians, for example, he hints at conflict between himself and Cephas (one of the original apostles, also known as Peter) and Apollos (a charismatic preacher who had gained a following in Corinth). In 2 Corinthians, he refers sarcastically to "super-apostles" who are questioning his own credentials as an apostle. In Galatians, he rails against people who are insisting that Christ-believers must also adhere to at least some of the provisions of the Jewish Torah ("Law"); here, he goes so far as to suggest that those who insist on circumcision for Gentile members of the church should go all the way and castrate themselves (Gal 5:12). Repeatedly, Paul insists, despite opinions to the contrary, that he is an "apostle" (that is, an authorized spokesperson for the Christian faith).[8]

Paul continued to be a controversial figure after his death. For example, the second-century "heretic" Marcion regarded him as the *only* true apostle of Christ, insisting that all of the other apostles had misunderstood Christ and his message.* At the other extreme, certain Jewish-Christians branded him "Satan's Apostle," maintaining that he had corrupted the original message of Jesus.[9] It appears that the book of Acts was intended, at least in part, to show that neither of these characterizations of Paul was accurate—that he was indeed a great Christian missionary but that he not only was in complete accord with the original apostles but was, in fact, subordinate to them.

The debate regarding Paul continues even into modern times. Some have asserted that Paul transformed Jesus' simple message of loving God and loving one's neighbor into an elaborate mythological drama of cosmic salvation, from the religion *of* Jesus into

---

*Marcion was a charismatic figure who not only regarded Paul as the only true apostle but also drew a distinction between the creator God of the Hebrew Scriptures and the redeemer God and Father of Jesus and accepted only ten letters of Paul and a version of the Gospel of Luke (different from what became the canonical gospel) as Scripture.

a religion *about* Jesus,[10] while others have insisted that he simply spelled out the post-resurrection implications of Jesus' message and activity.[11] Today, some maintain that Paul was misogynistic and/or homophobic, while others see him as radically egalitarian; some maintain that he was anti-Semitic, while others see him as a devout Jew who never rejected his Jewish heritage, faith, and practice; and the list goes on and on.

When people learn that I am a retired university professor, they typically ask me, "What did you teach?" When I tell them that I taught religion, they sometimes ask me what my specific area was within the study of religion. When I mention the letters of Paul, I often get an immediate response something like this: "Oh, I don't like Paul!" Sometimes this is said somewhat apologetically, the idea apparently being, "I know I *ought* to like Paul, but I just *don't*." At other times, however, it is said quite belligerently, with the implied question, why in the world would you want to study *that man's* letters? When I ask these people *why* they don't like Paul, I get a variety of answers. Some are quite *specific*: he accepted the institution of slavery; he called for unquestioning obedience to civil authorities; he was homophobic, misogynistic, and/or anti-Semitic. Others are more *general*: he was narrow-minded, prejudiced, stubborn, dogmatic, and/or obtuse; he was too different from Jesus; or simply, "I don't know *why*, but I just don't like him." The bottom line appears to be that Paul is simply not a "warm, fuzzy" apostle!

I am convinced, however, that some of the animosity toward Paul stems from the fact that, if people are reading Paul's letters at all, they are not reading them carefully enough, they are interpreting them on the basis of certain preconceived notions about Paul, they are not taking into account the cultural context in which the letters were written, and/or they are unaware of some of the conclusions of modern scholarship regarding the letters. I suggest, therefore, that a careful reading of the letters—without presuppositions insofar as this is possible and in the light of both the cultural context of the letters and the conclusions of modern scholarship—will uncover a number of surprises and that some of these surprises may help not only in reducing or perhaps even eliminating some of the animosity toward Paul but also in resolving certain of the controversies regarding Paul and his letters.

This book is not intended, however, as an apology for Paul (indeed, it is possible that some of the material in the book may make him *less* rather than *more* likeable). My purpose is simply to call attention to a few of the surprises that a careful, scholarly reading of his letters reveals and thus, hopefully, to present a more accurate picture of Paul and his letters than has typically been assumed. I could have included some other surprises. For example, I could have written chapters entitled "Paul on the Kingdom of God" (unlike Jesus in the synoptic Gospels, he says *very* little about it), "Paul on Judaism" (he *never* rejects his Jewish heritage, *always* regards himself as a devout Jew, and insists that "all Israel will be saved"), or "Paul on the Conduct of Christian Worship" (for example, he not only accepts the practice of "speaking in tongues" but even declares that he can do it better than anyone else). The surprises I have selected for inclusion, however, are ones that I regard as both interesting and important.

In the Introduction, I shall offer some preliminary observations that I regard as crucial for a proper understanding of the letters of Paul. There may well be some surprises there. In the chapters that follow, I shall discuss ten of what I regard as the most interesting and important surprises relating to Paul's letters. And so, I invite the reader to be prepared for some surprises from Paul.

Introduction

SOME PRELIMINARY OBSERVATIONS

Before looking at some surprises from Paul, it is important to bear in mind certain preliminary observations about Paul's letters in general. Some of these observations may themselves come as a surprise, and if so, they will fit comfortably under the heading, "Some Surprises from the Apostle Paul." One or two of the observations, however, are so obvious that it might appear unnecessary even to mention them. Nevertheless, all of these observations—and their implications—are important for understanding Paul's letters.

Preliminary Observation One

- The letters of Paul were not written for us.

The first preliminary observation clearly comes under the heading of the obvious, and it was articulated beautifully a number of years ago in the comic strip *Peanuts*. Charlie Brown encounters Linus, who is wearing a coat and tie and holding a book in his hand. Charlie Brown asks Linus, "Where have you been?" Linus replies, "Church school. We've been studying the letters of the Apostle Paul." Charlie Brown observes, "That should be interesting." Linus responds, "It is, although I must admit it makes me feel a little guilty. I always feel like I'm reading someone else's mail." And Linus was right! When we read Paul's letters, we *are* reading someone else's mail. Thus, the first preliminary observation is this: The letters of Paul were not written for us, nor were they written for people like us. Although this observation is obvious, some of its implications for understanding the letters are often overlooked.

The letters of Paul were written almost two thousand years ago, on the other side of the globe, in a foreign language, to people whose worldview and general outlook on life were quite different from ours. There is a huge gap—we might even say a chasm—between us and Paul's letters, and it is not just a chronological, geographical, and linguistic gap; it is also a scientific, philosophical, and cultural gap.

Most of us are well aware of the chronological and geographical gap, but it may be that the linguistic gap is often not taken seriously enough. Paul's letters were not written in English; they were written in Greek—not modern Greek but the *koinē* or "common" Greek that was the *lingua franca* of the eastern part of the Roman Empire in the first century (and the difference between this Greek and modern Greek is at least as great as the difference between the English of William Shakespeare and modern English). Most people must read Paul's letters in translation, and this means that they are not actually reading *Paul's letters*; what they are reading is somebody's *translation* of Paul's letters. And translation is, of course, a highly subjective and inexact undertaking; it is an art, not a science. One can never be certain how best to render the ancient idiom in the current vernacular, and this means that translation is always and inevitably an *interpretation*. Even those of us who can read *koinē* Greek are actually translating the letters from Greek into English—and thus interpreting them—in our own minds because Greek is not our native language and we don't actually *think* in Greek, at least not in any native and spontaneous way. In short, we simply have no immediate and direct access to Paul's letters in the way the original recipients of these letters did. We encounter the letters only through someone's (either our own or someone else's) translation—that is, interpretation—of them. Therefore, the linguistic gap between us and the letters is really quite formidable! And, incidentally, this is why it is a good idea to consult more than one translation when reading Paul's letters. This at least provides more than just *one* translation/interpretation of the Greek.

It is also important to note the scientific, philosophical, and cultural gap. There are many aspects of this gap, but one is par-

ticularly important. It was the German scholar Rudolf Bultmann*
who, more than seven decades ago, most pointedly called it to
the attention of scholars and, eventually, to many educated laypeople. According to Bultmann, the New Testament documents
(including Paul's letters) presuppose, reflect, and express what he
called an ancient "mythological" worldview—a worldview that is
radically different from what he termed the modern "scientific"
worldview. The major difference between the two worldviews is
that the modern scientific worldview assumes a *natural* cause for
everything that happens while the ancient mythological worldview is open to the possibility and even the likelihood of *super-
natural* causes. This means that, for the mythological worldview,
such things as angelic visitations, possession by demons, virgin
births, miraculous healings, resuscitations from the dead, and the
like might be unusual and even surprising, but they certainly were
not thought of as impossible or contrary to the laws of nature. But
for most of us, with our scientific worldview, things are different.
For example, most of us would be more than a little surprised if
we were to open our newspaper and see a headline reading, "God
Smites Wicked City with Hurricane." But for the writers of the
New Testament this would not be a problem at all, because for
them the universe was open and susceptible to just such super-
natural interventions. In other words, most modern people simply do not understand the workings of the universe in the same
way that the ancient writers of the New Testament did. Thus, if
we are to understand and respond positively to the message of
the New Testament, we must recognize this fact and somehow
get beyond (or behind) what Bultmann called the mythological
framework of the New Testament to the real heart of the gospel. In
short, the New Testament must be "demythologized" if it is to be
meaningful, believable, and compelling in the modern world. For
Bultmann, however, demythologizing the New Testament did not
mean *eliminating* the mythological features of the New Testament;
it meant *interpreting* them. Bultmann's question was this: How

*Bultmann (1884–1976) is generally regarded as the leading New Testament
scholar of the twentieth century.

can *we,* in terms of *our* worldview, say the same things that *they,* in terms of *their* worldview, were attempting to say? And he was convinced that the mythological elements in the New Testament could in fact be demythologized. For example, the "virgin birth" of Jesus could be viewed not as a biological statement about how Mary became pregnant but rather as an existential statement about the unique significance of Jesus.[1]

Regardless of what we may think about Bultmann and demythologizing, however, we must keep in mind the fact that Paul's letters were not written for us or even for people like us: there is a huge gap between us and the letters—a chronological, geographical, linguistic, scientific, philosophical, and cultural gap. This means that if we are even to begin to understand these letters, we must recognize the gap and make a serious attempt to bridge it.

Preliminary Observation Two
- The letters of Paul are genuine letters.

The second preliminary observation is almost as obvious as the first, and it is this: the letters of Paul are genuine letters. They are not sermons or essays or philosophical treatises. They represent genuine correspondence between Paul and first-century Christ-believers from whom he was physically separated and with whom he wished to communicate. They were written to address specific questions, concerns, problems, opportunities, and other circumstances that had arisen in the churches and that Paul felt needed his attention. For this reason, they are often referred to as "occasional letters"—letters composed for certain very specific occasions in the lives of these first-century Christians.* They can also be characterized as "stop-gap" letters: they were intended to serve simply as a substitute for Paul's physical presence—to address matters in a preliminary way pending Paul's arrival at some point in the (hopefully near) future.

An important corollary of this observation is that, as letters, they represent *only one side* of a dialogue between Paul

---

*It is not clear when the terms "Christian" was first used, and its use here may be anachronistic. Nevertheless, I am using it (and "non-Christian") simply for the sake of convenience.

and his intended readers or hearers. They tell us what *Paul* has to say about the matters at hand, but at best they only *hint* at what the recipients may have been thinking, saying, or doing. In other words, Paul is responding to situations and circumstances about which we have little or no independent knowledge, and this makes it difficult for us to understand much of that he says. More than forty years ago, Colin M. Morris wrote a book entitled *Epistles to the Apostle*, with the subtitle *Tarsus—Please Forward*.[2] In this book, Morris composed letters that he supposed might have come *to* Paul from the various churches to which he wrote. He attempted to surmise what the specific questions, problems, or other circumstances might have been that prompted Paul to write his letters. It is a fascinating book, but for the most part it is pure guesswork. We simply do not know for certain what was going on in the churches to which Paul wrote his letters, or what was going on in the minds of individual Christians within these churches. We cannot be certain just what it was that Paul was responding to when he wrote the letters. And Paul himself might not have completely or accurately understood what was going on in the churches to which he wrote. All we really have is what Paul wrote. And because we do not have the other side of the dialogue, much of what Paul said is simply not clear to us today.

The fact that the letters of Paul are genuine *letters* also has a second corollary: these letters do not provide us with what we might call Paul's "systematic theology"—not even when we look at all of them. They do not give us an overall view of Paul's assumptions and beliefs—one that is comprehensive and logically consistent, something like John Calvin's *Institutes* or St. Thomas Aquinas' *Summa Theologica*. The letters address only those topics that Paul regards as germane to the issues immediately at hand, and they do so in ways that are rhetorically crafted to elicit some specified or implied response on the part of the readers. In short, the letters of Paul are real letters, written to first-century Christians in the Roman Empire, addressing specific questions, concerns, issues, and circumstances in first-century churches, and they must be read and understood as such.

A third corollary of the fact that these are real letters is that they were not all written (or dictated) at the same time; the time span from the earliest (almost certainly 1 Thessalonians) to the latest (perhaps Romans) is probably almost a full decade. And it appears that Paul's own views may have changed or developed during these years as he encountered different situations, underwent different experiences, and/or simply thought more deeply about certain matters. This is probably true, for example, with regard to his eschatology: in 1 Thessalonians, he obviously expects the return of Jesus within his own lifetime; in Philippians, however, he appears to be wrestling with the possibility or even likelihood that he will not live to see this happen.[3] And the same may be true regarding other aspects of his thought. Thus, it appears that Paul's thought *developed and was shaped* in large part as a response to the various circumstances, issues, and problems that he and the churches faced.

Preliminary Observation Three

- Paul's letters were not intended
  to be scripture.

The third preliminary observation about Paul's letters may be a little less obvious than the first two, but it follows from the first two and is no less certain. It is this: *Paul's letters were not intended to be scripture.* For Paul, as for the first Christians generally, "scripture" meant the Hebrew scriptures—what Christians now call "the Old Testament." It was only later that letters attributed to Paul, four of the numerous gospels that were in existence, and certain other early Christian writings came to be regarded as scripture. Furthermore, like other Christians of his day, Paul expected the return of Christ—if not immediately, certainly in the relatively near future. Thus, he certainly had no intimation that people would be reading and talking about his letters two thousand years later. Paul was writing for Christians *of his own day*—addressing *their* questions, problems, and concerns. He was *not* writing for us. This does not mean, of course, that we cannot read Paul's letters with great benefit—that we cannot at times find that we are in fact addressed by what Paul has written. But this was not what Paul himself had in mind when he wrote the letters. He was writings *letters* for his own time, not *scripture* for all time.

Preliminary Observation Four

• We do not have all of the letters that Paul wrote.

The fourth, fifth, and sixth preliminary observations are less obvious than the first three, and they involve some rather technical aspects of New Testament scholarship. The fourth observation is this: *we do not have all of the letters that Paul wrote.* It would probably be safe to assume this, simply on *a priori* grounds, but such an assumption is not necessary. In 1 Cor 5:9, Paul says, "I wrote to you in the letter not to associate with immoral people." He then goes on in verses 10 and 11 to clarify what he had written—explaining that the "immoral people" he had in mind were people who called themselves "Christians," not non-Christians. In other words, before Paul wrote what we know as 1 Corinthians, he had written an earlier letter to the Christians in Corinth. This letter has not survived, and we have no idea what became of it.[4] We also have no idea how many other letters Paul may have written that have not been preserved, nor do we know what became of these letters. They may even have been intentionally destroyed by people who found their contents in some way problematic. We have no idea what these other letters might have said, and we have no way of knowing whether, or to what extent, knowledge of these other letters might change our understanding of Paul and his thought. But the simple truth is that Paul wrote at least one letter that has not survived—and almost certainly more, perhaps many more. We have only *part* of Paul's correspondence with first-century Christians.

Preliminary Observation Five

• Some letters attributed to Paul were probably
  not written by him.

The fifth preliminary observation is in a way the opposite of the fourth. Number four was that we do not have all of Paul's letters. And number five is this: some of the letters attributed to Paul that we do have were probably not written by Paul. What we are talking about here is called "pseudonymity"—writing under a false name, a pseudonym. This was a rather common practice in ancient times. We have examples of it from the Greeks, the Romans, the Jews, and early Christians. We have, for example, what scholars call "3 Corinthians." It claims to be written by Paul, but it is not included in the New Testament, no reputable New Testament scholar thinks Paul was its author, and most people have never even heard of it. We also have what claims to be correspondence between Paul and the well-known Roman Stoic philosopher Seneca. It is widely agreed, however, that this correspondence was not written by Paul and Seneca.

Within the New Testament itself, a great many scholars have long been convinced that what we know as 2 Peter was not written by Peter, even though it bears his name. In fact, 2 Peter is often dated sometime around the middle of the second century—probably almost a hundred years after the death of Peter. But what about the letters attributed to Paul? Are any of these pseudonymous? The answer is almost certainly yes. Indeed, there appears to be a general consensus among mainline New Testament scholars that, of the thirteen letters in the New Testament attributed to Paul, only seven are almost certainly authentically Pauline in authorship: the seven are Romans, 1 Corinthians, 2 Corinthians, Galatians, Philippians, 1 Thessalonians, and Philemon. The so-called Pastoral Letters (1 Timothy, 2 Timothy, and Titus) are widely regarded as pseudonymous, as are Ephesians, Colossians, and 2 Thessalonians by smaller yet significant numbers of scholars.[5]

To be sure, the decision about whether Paul actually wrote (or, more likely, dictated) a particular letter that bears his name is a somewhat subjective decision, and scholars disagree about specific letters. The criteria for such a decision include considerations of vocabulary, literary style, ideational content, and what appears to be the historical context of the writing in question. Take, for example, the case of the Pastoral Letters—1 Timothy, 2 Timothy, and Titus. They claim to be by Paul, but their vocabulary is distinctively different from that of the undisputed letters, their literary style is distinctively different, some of their ideas are distinctively different, and they appear to reflect a later stage in the development of Christian thought and practice.

Because pseudonymity—writing under a false name— would appear dishonest to most of us, it is important to note that it might be practiced for a number of possible reasons. Of course, the motivation might be to deceive, and, in fact, Bart Ehrman has recently put forward a rather strong argument that this was almost always the case and that pseudonymity was severely frowned upon in the ancient world.[6] But there might be other motives. It might be simple modesty—an unwillingness to call attention to oneself. It might also be the desire to pay honor to some important figure from the past or to apply the ideas of such a figure to new situations and problems—or, "What would Paul say about this if he were still alive?"—and it might be some combination of such motivations. My own judgment is that pseudonymous letters attributed to Paul were probably written by people who greatly respected and admired Paul, who saw him as a great pioneer of the faith, and who wanted to speak, in his name, to a new situation and a new set of issues.

The decision that a particular letter attributed to Paul is pseudonymous does not necessarily mean (a) that the letter does not at some points reflect *indirectly* the thinking of Paul, (b) that it is without value, (c) that it should be taken out of the New Testament, or (d) that it should simply be disregarded. It does mean, however, that we should not use this letter in any attempt to reconstruct the thought of *Paul*. The point is this: just as we do not have all of the letters composed by Paul, some of the letters attributed to Paul that we do have were probably not written by Paul, and the relation between the content of these letters and the thinking of Paul is problematic to say the least.

Preliminary Observation Six

- We do not have originals of any of Paul's letters.

The sixth and final preliminary observation is a bit complicated: we do not have any of the individual letters exactly as they came directly from the hand (or, more likely, the mouth) of Paul in the middle of the first century; we have them only as they were preserved, copied by hand, transmitted, assembled into a collection, and edited by early Christians sometime during the late first and the second centuries. This observation involves a number of points: *First*, we do not have the original—what scholars call the "autograph"—of any of the letters. Except for fragments, all that we have are hand-written copies, dating from around the year 200 and later—well more than a century after the time of Paul. No two of these copies read exactly the same, and we have no idea how far removed any of them may be from the originals. *Second,* we do not have early manuscripts of any *individual* letters; the earliest manuscripts that we have are all *collections* of letters. In short, we have the letters only in the form in which they were assembled and published by early Christians. *Third,* as already noted, these collections do not include all of the letters that were written by Paul, and they include some letters that almost certainly were not written by Paul. For example, they generally include the book of Hebrews, which almost no scholar today thinks was written by Paul (it doesn't even *claim* Pauline authorship!). *Fourth,* these collections of letters were assembled by early Christians, perhaps beginning as early as the late first century. It was these early Christians who decided what should be included and what should be left out, and we do not know exactly why or how they made the decisions they made.

A *fifth* point is also important: these early Christians almost certainly did some editing of the letters as they assembled them to form the collections that they published under Paul's name. Indeed, Leander C. Keck, formerly Dean of Yale Divinity School and a world-renowned New Testament scholar, has observed that "of the seven undoubtedly genuine letters, only in the case of Philemon can we be certain that what we have is virtually identical with what Paul wrote."[7]

One of the ways in which early Christians apparently edited the letters of Paul was to combine parts of originally separate letters to form what we now know as single letters. In other words, some of the letters in the collection appear to be composite letters. It has already been noted, for example, that 2 Cor 6:14-7:1 may be part of the earlier letter referred to in 1 Cor 5:9–10.[8] Moreover, many scholars think that what we know as "2 Corinthians" is actually a combination of parts of at least two originally different letters—part of one letter being found in chapters 1 through 9 and part of the other in chapters 10 through 13. Some scholars, however, find parts of as many as six originally separate letters in 2 Corinthians.[9] Another example is Philippians. Many scholars think it is composed of parts of either two or three originally different letters.[10] Yet another example: some scholars think that Romans originally ended with chapter 15 and that chapter 16 was originally part of a separate letter, probably addressed to Christians in Ephesus. Finally, a few scholars have divided 1 Corinthians into as few as two letters or as many as five different letter fragments. In short, some of what we now know as single letters may actually be compilations of parts of two or more originally separate letters—that is, composite letters. We have no idea why such "composite letters" might have been created. It may be that only fragments of certain letters had been preserved and that, if these fragments were to be included in a collection of Paul's *letters*, it would have been necessary to combine them with other fragments to form what appear to be *letters*. The manner in which parts of the separate letters were combined, however, may at times obscure the actual thought of Paul.

Another example of editing involves what are called "interpolations"—adding new non-Pauline material to the older Pauline material in much the same way as ancient Hebrew writers appear to have added material to such writings as Isaiah, Jeremiah, and Ezekiel.* There almost certainly are some non-Pauline interpolations in the Pauline letters. Even some very conservative scholars recognize this. Gordon C. Fee, for example, has argued that 1 Cor 14:34–35 is a later addition to the text of the letter (this is the infamous passage that forbids women to speak in church). He bases his argument essentially on six types of data: vocabulary, literary style, ideational content, apparent historical context, the fact that the verses appear at two different locations in various manuscripts, and the fact that they appear to break the context or the flow of the argument in what Paul is writing to the Corinthians. In short, according to Fee (and many others), 1 Cor 14:34–35 was probably added later by someone other than Paul.[11] Similar arguments have been made regarding a rather large number of passages. Sixteen years ago, I published a book entitled *Interpolations*

---

*If, as a majority of New Testament scholars think, Mark was the earliest of the gospels and served as a major source for both Matthew and Luke, then these latter two gospels could be viewed as *versions of Mark with material (that is, interpolations) added*.

in the Pauline Letters, in which I argued that four passages—1 Cor 11:3–16; 2:6–16; 1 Corinthians 13; and Rom 1:18–2:29—are later additions.[12] More recently, I have argued in print that four other passages—Gal 2:7b–8; 1 Cor 15:29–34; Rom 8:29–30; and 2 Cor 3:7–18—are also interpolations.[13] In my earlier book, I also summarized the arguments of other scholars who regard Rom 16:25–27; 2 Cor 6:14–7:1; 1 Thess 2:13–16; Rom 13:1–7; and 1 Cor 10:1–22 as interpolations.[14] And there are almost certainly more; in fact, J. C. O'Neill argued some years ago that both Romans and Galatians are literally full of non-Pauline interpolations.[15] Few scholars would go as far as O'Neill, but it is widely agreed, at least in principle, that the letters of Paul are likely to contain at least some non-Pauline additions. Some of these interpolations may have been added at the time when the letters were assembled and published in collections, but some may well have appeared at earlier stages in the transmission of the letters.[16]

What this all comes down to is that the people who collected and edited the letters of Paul had to make a number of what we might call editorial decisions: (1) They had to decide which letters to include in their collections and which to omit. (2) When the wording of various manuscripts differed, they had to decide which wording to follow. (3) They had to decide whether to combine parts of originally separate letters to form what now appear to be single letters. (4) They had to decide whether to delete any material from the letters. (5) They had to decide whether any materials, either Pauline or non-Pauline, should be added to any of the letters. All of this means that when we study the letters today, we need to be aware of such editorial decisions and take them seriously into account as we attempt to understand the thought of Paul.

Conclusion

The overall thrust of the six preliminary observations is the following: what we have before us, as we set out to study the content of the Pauline letters, is a collection of hand-written documents that were preserved, copied by hand, transmitted, assembled, edited, and attributed to Paul by early Christians a generation or more after the lifetime of Paul. The letters were not written for us, they were written long ago in a distant part of the world in a foreign language, and they reflect an alien worldview and culture. They are really and truly genuine letters, not intended by Paul to become scripture. We do not have all of them, some of the ones we do have were almost certainly not written by Paul, and all of them have been edited in various ways by early Christians. And finally, as time passed Paul may have changed his mind about some matters, or at least revised his thinking. All of this greatly complicates the task of trying to decide what Paul thought about any given topic.

In this book, I shall be assuming Pauline authorship of only *seven* of the letters that bear Paul's name: 1 Thessalonians, 1 Corinthians, 2 Corinthians, Philippians, Philemon, Galatians, and Romans. In my judgment, the others—1 Timothy, 2 Timothy, Titus, Ephesians, Colossians, and 2 Thessalonians—are pseudonymous. In addition, I shall be assuming that even the seven authentically Pauline letters have been *edited* by early Christians in the various ways indicated above, including the addition of interpolations. In all fairness, I must acknowledge that some of the surprises that follow would disappear if all thirteen of the letters bearing Paul's name were regarded as authentically Pauline and if proposed interpolations were viewed as Pauline (in particular, chapter 6 would either disappear or be radically altered).

Paul on the
Historical Jesus

The Surprise

- Paul's letters say almost nothing about the historical Jesus.

When we read the letters of Paul, one of the first and most obvious surprises that strikes us is the fact that there is almost nothing in these letters about the life and teaching of the historical Jesus. Many years ago, Rudolf Bultmann, arguably the most important New Testament scholar of the twentieth century, wrote the following: "[Paul's] letters barely show traces of . . . tradition concerning the history and preaching of Jesus. All that is important for him in the story of Jesus is the fact that Jesus was born a Jew and lived under the Law . . . and that he had been crucified."[1] This may be a little too sketchy, but it isn't far off the mark. All we can get about the historical Jesus from Paul's letters is the following:

First, Paul says that Jesus was a Jew (Gal 4:4; Rom 9:5; see also Rom 15:8), but this is pretty obvious; so far as I am aware, about the only people who have ever denied that Jesus was Jewish were some of the Nazis in the 1930s and 1940s.

Second, Paul says that Jesus "was descended from David" (Rom 1:3), but this may be more of a theological affirmation than a historical fact: in the minds of some, the Messiah was *supposed* to be a "son of David," so Paul, like some other early Christians, may have simply assumed that *because* Jesus was the Messiah he *must* have been descended from David.

Third, Paul indicates that Jesus had a human birth (Phil 2:7b), that he was "born of a woman," and was "born under the law" (Gal 4:4). This means simply (a) that he was human, (b) that, like all humans, he was born, (c) that, like all humans, he had a mother (who is not named), and (d) that he was a Jew.

Fourth, Paul indicates in one place that Jesus had two or more "brothers" who were married, but he fails to give their names (1 Cor 9:5), and in another place he identifies a man named James as "the Lord's brother" (Gal 1:19).

Fifth, Paul appears to be aware that Jesus had twelve particularly close followers (1 Cor 15:5), of whom he names James and Cephas and John (1 Cor 15:5; Gal 1:18; 2:9).[2]

Sixth, Paul refers to Jesus being "betrayed" or "handed over" and reports that on the night of his "betrayal" he instituted what we now know as the "Lord's Supper" (1 Cor 11:23–25).

Seventh, Paul says that Jesus "humbled himself and became obedient to the point of death—even death on a cross" (Phil 2:8). And then, of course, there are numerous other passages that speak of the death of Jesus, even specifying that it was death by crucifixion.

And this is all we have in the letters of Paul regarding what we might call the biographical facts of the life of Jesus: He was a Jew, descended from David, with a human mother and a human birth. He had at least two married brothers, one of whom was named James. He had certain close followers. He was betrayed or handed over. On the night of his "betrayal" he instituted what we know as the Lord's Supper. And he was put to death by crucifixion. That's it!*

In addition to this, to be sure, there are a few passages that attribute certain *virtues* to Jesus such as obedience (Rom 5:18–19), meekness and gentleness (2 Cor 10:1a), compassion (Phil 1:8), humility and obedience (Phil 2:6–11), and the like (see, for example, Rom 15:3; 2 Cor 8:9). It is far from clear, however, that these passages refer to the historical Jesus at all; they may have in mind either the preexistent Christ or the resurrected and exalted Lord.

---

*References to Jesus' resurrection are not included because *resurrection* is not something that the historian can investigate; it is a matter of *faith*, not *history*.

I find it significant that, although there are a number of points at which a reference to the teaching of Jesus might have bolstered his own argument,[3] only rarely does Paul invoke what he calls "a word of the Lord" in setting forth his own teaching. He does so in 1 Cor 7:10–11, where he is talking about marriage and divorce; in 1 Cor 9:14, where he is talking about material compensation for those who proclaim the gospel; in 1 Cor 11:24–25, where he is talking about the Last Supper; and in 1 Thess 4:15, where he is talking about the expected return of Jesus. Only in the next to last case, however, does the statement of Paul correspond exactly with anything we find in the gospels, and, in the other cases, it is unclear whether Paul has in mind words of the historical Jesus or what he regards as revelations from the risen Christ.

In a very few passages, there may be verbal reminiscences of the teaching of Jesus: In 1 Thess 5:2, Paul says that "the day of the Lord will come like a thief in the night" (see Matt 24:43–44 and Luke 12:39–40); in Rom 12:14, he says, "Bless those who persecute you; bless and do not curse them" (see Matt 5:44); in Rom 13:9–10, he says, "The commandments . . . are summed up in this word, 'Love your neighbor as yourself'" (see Mark 12:31; Matt 22:39; Luke 10:27); in Rom 14:14, he says, "Nothing is unclean in itself, but it is unclean for anyone who thinks it is unclean" (see Mark 7:15); in Rom 16:19b, he says, "I want you to be wise in what is good and guileless in what is evil" (see Matt 10:16); and in 1 Cor 13:2b, he says, "and if I have all faith, so as to remove mountains, but do not have love, I am nothing" (see Matt 17:20; 21:21; Mark 11:23; Luke 17:6). I should note, though, that Paul himself never attributes any of this material to Jesus, and much of it may simply have been a common staple in the tradition and preaching of the early church; thus, it may not reflect any specific knowledge about the historical Jesus at all. It is also likely that one or more of the gospel writers were familiar with one or more of the Pauline letters and placed Pauline-like statements on the lips of the historical Jesus—in other words, that materials in the gospels reflect materials in Paul's letters rather than *vice versa*.

When you look at what has been summarized, it may initially appear that it tells us a great deal about the historical Jesus. But look at *what we do not have:* nothing about Jesus' birth beyond the simple fact that he was born of an unnamed woman and born under the Law; nothing about his family except that he had two or more married brothers, one of whom was named James; nothing about Jesus' baptism by John the Baptist (in fact, nothing about John the Baptist at all); nothing about Jesus' temptations in the wilderness; nothing about his proclamation of the coming of the Kingdom of God (in fact, another surprise is that the idea of the Kingdom of God receives very little attention in the letters of Paul); nothing about Jesus' call for repentance;[4] nothing about his teaching in parables, and little if anything about the actual content of his teaching; nothing about his choosing of the apostles; nothing about the Transfiguration; nothing about him casting out demons, or healing people with various afflictions, or raising people from the dead, or performing other types of "miracles"; nothing about Jesus associating with tax-collectors, prostitutes, and other "sinners"; nothing about his conflicts with the Jewish religious leaders; nothing about the Triumphal Entry or cleansing of the Temple; nothing regarding the circumstances surrounding his arrest, trial, and crucifixion. And the list could go on and on. After surveying all of the relevant materials, James D. G. Dunn summarizes the matter as follows:

> In short, Paul tells us next to nothing about the life and ministry of Jesus apart from its climactic finale. Had we possessed only Paul's letters, it would be impossible to say much about Jesus of Nazareth, let alone even to attempt a life of Jesus. Paul makes it clear that Jesus was a Jew. And that is a crucially important fact. But beyond that the life of Jesus seems to be little more than an assumed and hidden antecedent to the all-important record of his death.[5]

Some Possible Reasons for the Surprise

Following his summary, Dunn raises the question, "What are we to make of this for an appreciation of Paul's gospel and theology?"[6] And this is the question that is now to be explored: Why is it that Paul tells us so *very* little about the life and teaching of the historical Jesus? The short answer, of course, is that we simply do not know. Nevertheless, several possible answers have been suggested.

The most common answer is that Paul simply thought it unnecessary to say very much in his letters about the life and teaching of Jesus because he could presuppose that his readers already knew the basic facts—either because he himself had given them this information while he was living and working in their midst or because they had gotten it from some other source. In either case, there would be no need for Paul to repeat in his letters what his readers already knew. Marcus J. Borg,* for example, insists that Paul *must* have talked about the life and teaching of Jesus as a regular part of his evangelistic preaching. Speaking of Paul's initial contact with the woman named Lydia in the city of Philippi (Acts 16:11–15), Borg writes:

> Paul would have told her that Jesus was the messiah. But for this to mean anything to her, he would also have had to tell her about the kind of person Jesus was. Otherwise, the claim that Jesus was the messiah would have been a cipher, a claim without content. Thus, I assume that what Jesus was like—his subversive wisdom, his healings, his passion for social justice for the poor and marginalized, his indictment of the domination system, his goodness—mattered to Paul and would have been central to his message.[7]

My own judgment, however, is that Borg's statement is unconvincing for at least four reasons. In the first place, for Borg to say that Jesus *must* have talked about the life and teaching of Jesus really means little more than that *Borg himself*, if *he* had been in Paul's position, would have talked about the life and teaching of Jesus. In other words, Borg thinks Paul *should* have talked about the life and teaching of Jesus. But we certainly do not know that Paul *did* in fact talk about the life and teaching of Jesus when he was present in the churches; he may have, but we do not know this.

In the second place, Borg's argument is unconvincing because Paul had never even been to at least one of the places to which he wrote a letter. He had never been to Rome, but he wrote a long letter to the church there, and in this letter, as in the other letters, he said almost nothing about the life and teaching of Jesus.

*Borg (1942–2015), a well-known Jesus scholar and popular writer and lecturer, was one of the founding members of the Jesus Seminar.

In the third place, Borg's argument is unconvincing because Paul could certainly have presupposed that his readers already knew about the death, resurrection, and expected return of Jesus. Nevertheless, he talks a great deal in the letters particularly about the death and resurrection and to some extent also about the return. Why, then, does he say so little in the letters about the life and teaching of Jesus? The reason must have been something other than the fact that he simply presupposed that his readers already knew all they needed to know about this.

In the fourth place, Borg's argument is unconvincing because, as already noted, there are a number of places in the letters where an appeal to a saying of Jesus could clearly have bolstered Paul's own argument. To cite just one example, when Paul talks in chapters 8–10 of 1 Corinthians about whether Christians are permitted to eat meat from animals that have been sacrificed in pagan rituals, or when he talks in chapter 14 of Romans about what Christians may or may not eat and drink, he could have greatly strengthened his argument if he had simply quoted the reported words of Jesus: "It is not what goes into the mouth that defiles a person, but it is what comes out of the mouth that defiles" (Matt 15:11).[8] Other examples include Paul's teaching about the supreme importance of love (Rom 13:8–10 and elsewhere), not seeking vengeance (Rom 12:14–21), and not judging one another (Rom 14:10–13). In each case, Paul could have strengthened his own position by appealing to a statement of Jesus, but he failed to do this. Thus, it appears unlikely that Paul refrained from talking about Jesus' life and teaching simply because he could presuppose that his readers already knew about the basic facts.

And this leads to *the second answer* that is sometimes given to the question of why there is so little information about the historical Jesus in the letters of Paul. It is this: in view of the overarching centrality of the cross and resurrection in Paul's thinking, everything else simply paled into relative insignificance—including the life and teaching of the historical Jesus. As Paul himself put it in 1 Cor 2:2: "I decided to know nothing among you except Jesus Christ, and him crucified." For Paul, what really mattered about Jesus was the fact of his death and resurrection and, to a somewhat lesser extent, the expectation of his return. To focus on the life and teaching of Jesus would really have been something of a distraction.

There would appear to be a great deal of truth in this second answer. And if such a lack of interest in the life and teaching of Jesus strikes one as a bit strange, it should be noted that the best-known of all Christian confessions, the Apostles' Creed, shows at least an equal lack of interest in the life and teaching of the historical Jesus. How does the part about Jesus go? "I believe . . . in Jesus Christ, his only son, our Lord, who was conceived by the Holy Spirit, born of the virgin Mary"—and then what comes next?— "suffered under Pontius Pilate, was crucified dead and buried." Birth, then suffering and death—nothing at all in between. Nothing about what he did or what he said or what happened to him between his birth and his death. Apparently, in some versions of early Christianity, what Jesus did and said and what happened to him between his birth and death were considered relatively unimportant when compared with the cross, resurrection, and expected return. And this appears to have been the case with Paul. So, this may be at least part of the reason why Paul says so very little about the life and teaching of the historical Jesus in his letters.

But there is yet *a third answer* that is sometimes given to the question of why there is so little in the letters of Paul about the life and teaching of Jesus. This third answer may initially appear rather unlikely, but, in my judgment, it cannot simply be dismissed out of hand. The third answer is this: Paul *says* very little in his letters about the life and teaching of Jesus because he actually *knows* very little about the life and teaching of the historical Jesus.

After all, Paul was not one of the followers of Jesus during Jesus' lifetime, and it is almost certain that he never even came into contact with the historical Jesus. Thus, he would have had very little if any personal basis for knowledge about the life and teaching of Jesus. Furthermore, none of the gospels had yet been written, and so Paul could not have gotten information about Jesus from them. Finally, judging strictly from Paul's own letters, it would appear that he spent very little time in or around Jerusalem; most of the time he was in Syria or what is now Turkey or Greece. Indeed, in Gal 1:15–23 he emphasizes the fact that he has had minimal contact with the people who actually knew Jesus during his lifetime, insisting in Gal 1:12 that the gospel he preached came to him not from a human but rather "through a revelation of Jesus Christ." In short, it may well be the case that Paul actually knew very little about the life and teaching of the historical Jesus, and this is at least part of the reason why he says so little about the historical Jesus in his letters.

Another Suggestion

By way of summary, there appear to be *three* possible reasons why Paul says so little in his letters about the life and teaching of the historical Jesus: (1) he could simply presuppose that his readers already knew the basic facts, (2) he himself was much less interested in the *biographical* facts than he was in Jesus' death, resurrection, and expected return, and/or (3) he actually knew very little about the life and teaching of the historical Jesus. There may, however, be yet *a fourth possible reason* why there is so little about the life and teaching of Jesus in the letters of Paul. Paul may have had a *theological* reason for not talking about the life and teaching of Jesus.

For Paul, "justification"—being in a right relationship with God—is not something that can be "earned" by good conduct. The classic statement of his position is found in Gal 2:16, which is typically translated somewhat as follows: "We know that a person is justified not by works of law but through faith in Jesus Christ. And we have put our faith in Christ Jesus, so that we might be justified by faith in Christ, and not by works of law, because no one will be justified by works of law."[9] What does Paul mean by "works of law"? James D. G. Dunn and some others have recently argued that he is referring simply to those parts of the Jewish Law that distinguished between Jews and Gentiles: circumcision, the food laws, and Sabbath observance (the so-called "boundary markers"). But others, and I include myself among their number, think that Paul is speaking of the Jewish Law as a whole—keeping the commandments of God as set forth in Torah. People are not justified—brought into a right relationship with God—by following the commandments contained in Torah. By extension, though, "law" might refer to *any* standard of behavior by which people evaluate their own conduct in an attempt to determine whether they measure up to what is expected or required of them or by which they expect to be judged by someone else. And "works" might refer to their attempts to "measure up." Thus, Paul can refer to "works" in talking about Abraham, who, according to the Hebrew scriptures, lived long before the Torah was given to Moses (Rom 4:1–5). In short, as Marcus J. Borg puts it, "Life under the law is the life of 'measuring up,' in which our well being depends upon how well we do . . . Life under the law is . . . living according to the 'performance principle.'"[10] And this is what Paul opposes. For him, *justification* is a *gift* from God, not a *reward* for good conduct.

The point here is that the teaching and example of Jesus might easily become "law," and human attempts to follow the teaching and example of Jesus might easily become "works of law." There are certainly people in our own time, as in times past, who would argue that being a Christian is essentially a matter of "following the teaching and example of Jesus." For them, the life and teaching of Jesus have become in effect a new law by which they evaluate their own behavior in an attempt to determine whether they measure up or by which they expect to be judged by someone else (for example, God). The "good Christian"—the one who pleases God—is the one who follows the teaching and example of Jesus in his or her own daily life. Those who do not do so cannot be regarded as good Christians no matter how strong their faith or how conscientious their attention to matters of sound doctrine and devout worship. Some of you may remember the very popular book of an earlier generation entitled, *In His Steps,* with the subtitle, *What Would Jesus Do?,* written by Charles M. Sheldon.[11] Its view of Christianity is, in every situation, to ask what Jesus would do and then to act accordingly. According to Sheldon, this is what being a Christian is all about!

In the New Testament, such a view of Christianity is set forth in the book of James, which says that "a person is justified by works and not by faith alone" (2:24). Here, it is clear that "works" does not refer specifically to Torah, because the examples given are clothing and feeding the needy (verses 14–17), Abraham offering his son on the altar (verses 21–24), and Rahab the harlot harboring the Israelite messengers (verse 25). "Works" refers simply to human conduct. Along somewhat different lines, the Gospel of Matthew insists that the Jewish Law is still in effect and that the teaching of Jesus is the authoritative interpretation of this Law. Specifically, Matthew insists upon the following: Jesus did not come to abolish the Law, but rather to fulfill it (5:17–18); whoever breaks one of the least of the commandments and teaches others to do so will be called least in the Kingdom of Heaven, and whoever keeps the commandments and teaches others to do so will be called great in the Kingdom of Heaven (5:19); and unless the righteousness of Jesus' followers *exceeds* that of the scribes and Pharisees, they will never enter the Kingdom of Heaven (5:21). The scribes and Pharisees were the people who scrupulously sought to obey the will of God in all aspects of their lives—to follow Torah in all of its details. But the righteousness of Jesus' followers could *exceed* that of the scribes and Pharisees because, for the author of Matthew, it is precisely the teaching of Jesus that provides the true and authoritative interpretation of the Law (5:21–48). In other words, what is required, according to Matthew, is faithful obedience to the teaching of Jesus. And the teaching of Jesus thus becomes, in effect, the new *Law*—the new standard by which human behavior is to be measured.

For Paul, though, this would be simply another version of what he calls "works of law." For him, *justification*—being in a right relationship with God—is not a human achievement. It is not a matter of following the rules, no matter who makes the rules, whether Moses, Jesus, or even God. *Justification* is an act of God. It is not something that can be earned by good behavior, whether "good behavior" be defined in terms of the Jewish Law, the teaching and example of Jesus, or any other set of rules and regulations. Indeed, the difference between Paul and the Gospel of Matthew is strikingly illustrated by the fact that the same Greek work *(dikaiosynē)* is translated as "righteousness" in Matthew and as "justification" in the letters of Paul. For Matthew, *dikaiosynē* is a human *achievement;* for Paul, *dikaiosynē* a divine *gift.*

In short, Paul may have shied away from talking about the life and teaching of Jesus because he did not want people to see the teaching and example of Jesus either as *a new law* that would simply replace the Jewish Law or as *the authoritative interpretation* of the Jewish Law that would become the normative standard for Christian behavior. He did not want people to get the idea that they could somehow "earn" justification by being good—that is, by following the teaching and example of Jesus. And so, it is at least possible that Paul rarely mentioned the life and teaching of Jesus precisely because he feared that the teaching and example of Jesus would be seen as Law.

Summary and Conclusion

By way of summary and conclusion: (1) It *may* be the case that Paul said so little about the life and teaching of Jesus because he could presuppose knowledge regarding the historical Jesus on the part of his readers. (2) It *very well may* be the case that Paul himself actually knew very little about the life and teaching of the historical Jesus. (3) It surely *is* the case that Paul regarded the life and teaching of the historical Jesus as relatively unimportant in comparison with his death, resurrection, and expected return. Indeed, in my judgment, if Paul had known a fair amount about the life and teaching of Jesus, and if he had thought that this was important for Christian faith and life, he almost certainly would have included a great deal more information about the historical Jesus in his letters. Thus, it would appear either that Paul did not know very much about the life and teaching of Jesus or that he considered this relatively unimportant or that he had some other reason for saying so little about it. And at least a part of the reason may well have been his fear of turning the teaching and example of Jesus into a new law that people would slavishly endeavor to follow in an attempt to place themselves in a right relationship with God—a relationship that Paul calls *justification*. Before looking in chapter 3 at Paul's views regarding justification, however, it will be helpful to consider another surprise that may stem from his understanding of justification.

2

Paul on Repentance and Forgiveness

Christianity has typically placed a heavy emphasis on the need for repentance and forgiveness. For example, the following confession appears in the 1946 edition of the Presbyterian *Book of Common Worship*:

> We acknowledge and confess our manifold sins, which we, from time to time, most grievously have committed, by thought, word, and deed, against thy divine Majesty. We do earnestly repent, and are heartily sorry for these our misdoings; the remembrance of them is grievous unto us. Have mercy upon us, have mercy upon us, most merciful Father, for thy Son our Lord Jesus Christ's sake. Forgive us all that is past, and grant that we may hereafter serve and please thee in newness of life, to the honor and glory of thy name.

The underlying conviction here, of course, is that all of us are sinners in need of forgiveness and that the prerequisite for forgiveness is repentance. Thus, repentance and forgiveness are essential components in the process of salvation.

If we are to believe the synoptic Gospels (Matthew, Mark, and Luke), the emphasis on the need for *repentance* goes back to Jesus himself.* Both Mark and Matthew have Jesus begin his public ministry by calling for repentance (Mark 1:15; Matt 4:17).

---

*The Greek noun *metanoia* ("repentance") and the Greek verb *metanoein* ("to repent") refer literally to a change of one's mind or a change of thinking. By extension, however, they refer to "turning away" from one's former pattern of behavior.

Luke has Jesus identifying his mission as that of calling sinners to repentance (5:32) and speaking of the joy in heaven over a sinner who repents (15:7, 10). Both Matthew and Luke report Jesus' lamentation at the lack of repentance on the part of his hearers (Matt 11:20–21; 12:41; Luke 10:13; 11:32; 13:3, 5). Luke has Jesus command that "repentance . . . be preached in his name to all nations" (Luke 24:47). Repentance is absolutely essential!

The synoptic Gospels also make it clear that Jesus spoke of *forgiveness*. The matter is complicated, however, by the fact that the Greek words for "forgiveness" (*aphesis*) and "to forgive" (*aphienai*) have a rather wide range of other meanings. The root idea is that of "release," "liberation," "departure," or "removal," and a decision must be made in each individual case as to whether the specific notion of "forgiveness" is intended. With the meaning "forgiveness," the noun appears on Jesus' lips once in Mark (3:29), once in Matthew (26:28), and once in Luke (24:47).[1] With the meaning "to forgive," with reference to *God's* forgiveness, the verb appears on the lips of Jesus thirteen times in Matthew, seven times in Mark, and fourteen times in Luke.[2] Most notably, Luke's version of the Lord's Prayer includes the petition, "Forgive us our sins" (11:4).

Repentance and forgiveness are juxtaposed at Mark 1:4 and Luke 4:3, where John the Baptist proclaims "a baptism of *repentance* for the *forgiveness* of sins" and Luke 24:47, where Jesus commands his disciples to preach "*repentance* for the *forgiveness* of sins." Perhaps the classic New Testament statement regarding repentance and forgiveness is found in 1 John 1:8–9, which reads, "If we say we have no sin, we deceive ourselves, and the truth is not in us. If we confess our sins, he is faithful and just, and will forgive our sins and cleanse us from all unrighteousness" (here, "confess our sins" is the functional equivalent of "repent of our sins"). In other words, the basic human problem is that we are all sinners, that the only remedy for sin is forgiveness, and that the prerequisite for forgiveness is confession of one's sins and repentance.

The Surprise

• Paul's letters say virtually nothing about repentance or forgiveness.

But what about Paul? Does he speak of repentance and forgiveness? According to the book of Acts, he does call for repentance

(Acts 17:30; 20:21; 26:20). When we look at Paul's *letters*, however, we find, much to our surprise, that they have virtually nothing to say about repentance or forgiveness.

In the thirteen letters attributed to Paul, the noun "repentance" (*metanoia*) occurs only four times (including twice in the same passage), and the verb "to repent" (*metanoein*) occurs only once. The noun appears twice in 2 Cor 7:9–10, where Paul rejoices at the "repentance" of his readers (that is, their changed attitude toward him), but this says nothing directly about a change of attitude toward God, which is what is involved in the usual understanding of repentance. Otherwise, the noun appears only in 2 Tim 2:25, which almost certainly was not written by Paul,[3] and in Rom 2:4, which may not have been written by Paul.[4] The verb appears in 2 Cor 12:21, where Paul simply expresses the hope that those who have sinned will repent. Otherwise, there is nothing at all about repentance in the letters of Paul.

Paul also has almost nothing to say about forgiveness, which is generally understood as God's response to repentance. In the thirteen letters that bear his name, the noun "forgiveness" appears only twice and the verb "to forgive" only five times. Both of the occurrences of the noun (Col 1:14 and Eph 1:7) carry the meaning "forgiveness," but both are in writings that most likely were not written by Paul.[5] Thus, Paul himself probably did not use the noun at all. The verb, which, as already indicated, can have a rather wide range of meanings, has the meaning "to forgive" only once (Rom 4:7), and here Paul is simply quoting from Psalm 32:1. In short, the notion of forgiveness, like that of repentance, is almost totally absent from the letters of Paul.

The surprise, then, is this: the letters of Paul have virtually nothing to say about either repentance or forgiveness. Surely, this calls for some explanation!

Possible Explanations for the Surprise

One possible explanation is that Paul simply has a number of other metaphors for what James D. G. Dunn calls "The New Beginning."[6] And this is indeed the case! Paul speaks of "justification," "redemption," "deliverance" or "liberation," "reconciliation," "salvation," "adoption," and so on. It may be the case that Paul simply prefers these other metaphors and, because he does not speak of "forgiveness," neither does he talk about "repentance" because the two are almost inextricably connected. Nevertheless, the question must be posed as to *why* Paul prefers these other metaphors over "repentance" and "forgiveness."

A partial explanation may lie in Paul's rather unique understanding of "sin." The call for repentance assumes that the human condition apart from Christ is characterized by sin, and Paul would certainly agree with this assumption. Indeed, sin is a critically important issue in his letters. In his seven undisputedly authentic letters, the noun "sin" (either *hamartia* or *hamartēma* in Greek) appears some sixty-one times,[7] the noun "sinner" (*hamartōlos*) occurs six times,[8] and the verb "to sin" (*hamartanein*) is found fourteen times.[9] In addition, the noun "trespass" (*paraptōma*) appears eleven times.[10] In a number of these references, "sin" and "to sin" clearly refer to specific acts or attitudes that are contrary to the will of God.[11] When sin is understood in this way, a call for repentance is indeed appropriate, but, as already noted, such a call is almost completely absent from Paul's letters.

In Romans, however, which may well be Paul's latest surviving letter, "sin" often does *not* refer to individual acts of transgression. Rather, the word appears in the *singular* (sin), not the plural (sins), and it refers to *an alien power* by which humans are enslaved and from which they need liberation.[12] Paul speaks about sin coming into the world (Rom 5:12–13) and "dwelling" in people (Rom 7:17–20, 23); about people being "deceived" by sin (Rom 7:11), being "under the power of sin" (Rom 3:9), being "slaves" or "captives" to sin (Rom 6:6, 16–22; 7:23); and about sin "reigning" (Rom 5:21; 6:12) or "having dominion" (Rom 6:14). In these sections of Romans, therefore, sin is not so much the bad things that people *do* as it is the enslaving power that *causes* them to do wrong. In fact, we could almost say that "Sin" (singular and capitalized) here becomes Paul's functional equivalent of "Satan" or "the Devil."[13] Instead of saying, "The Devil made me do it," Paul would say, "Sin made me do it."[14] And so people *yield* themselves either to sin or to God (Rom 6:13); they are *slaves* either of sin or of God (Rom 6:20–22). With this understanding of sin, the remedy is not *repentance and forgiveness* but rather *deliverance* or *liberation*. Thus, Paul speaks of being "set free" from sin (Rom 5:18, 22; 8:2), not about having one's sins forgiven.

There may, however, be a still deeper reason why Paul has virtually nothing to say about repentance (and, by extension, about forgiveness): he may have found the very idea of repentance theologically problematic. Beverly R. Gaventa suggests that Paul avoids talk of repentance because repentance is something that people *do* in order to receive forgiveness—that is, to be brought into a right relationship with God.[15] *If* people repent, they will be forgiven. But notice the *if*. And it is the *if* that Paul no doubt would find theologically objectionable. With Paul, there is no *if*, because, as will be discussed in chapter 3, there is *nothing* that a person can *do* to attain a right relationship with God. This can only be brought about by God. In short, for Paul, it is not what *we* do that counts; it is what *God* does. And so, it may well be the case that Paul, unlike some of the other New Testament writers, avoids talking about repentance because repentance is something that people *do* in the hope of thereby attaining a right relationship with God.[16]

Addendum

Neither the noun "repentance" nor the verb "to repent" appears in the Gospel of John, and there is only one reference to "forgiveness" (John 20:23). Here, as at other points, we have probably been much too inclined to read both Paul's letters and the Gospel of John in light of other New Testament writings and have failed to allow them to stand in their own right as independent testimonies to the real *diversity* of early Christian faith.

Paul on Justification[1]

Background

The Protestant Reformation began when Martin Luther discovered what he understood to be the "true" meaning of Rom 1:17—a verse that is notoriously difficult to translate and understand. The New Revised Standard Version renders it: "For in it [that is, in the gospel] the righteousness of God is revealed through faith and for faith; as it is written, 'The one who is righteous will live by faith.'" A footnote, however, indicates that an alternative translation of the last part of the verse would read, "The one who is righteous through faith will live." Opting for this latter interpretation, Luther was convinced that a person becomes *righteous* or *justified*—that is, in a right relationship with God—by *faith*. Luther then applied this insight to other Pauline passages, particularly in Romans and Galatians, and thus was born the rallying cry of the Reformation: "Justification by Faith and Not by Works." The classic proof text for this is Gal 2:16, which the New Revised Standard Version translates as follows (emphasis mine):

> yet we know that a person is justified not by the works of the law but through *faith in Jesus Christ*. And *we have come to believe in Christ Jesus*, so that we might be justified by *faith in Christ* and not by doing the works of the law, because no one will be justified by the works of the law.[2]

Until recently, most New Testament scholars (particularly Protestant scholars) have concurred in Luther's understanding of Gal 2:16 and related texts,[3] and this, of course, is what most of us—at least most Protestants—were taught and have believed: according to Paul, a person is justified not by obeying the commandments but rather through faith in Christ.

The Surprise

What may come as a surprise, however, is the fact that there is now a vigorous debate among New Testament scholars regarding the correct translation of the italicized phrases in the above translation of Gal 2:16 and of the same or similar phrases elsewhere in Paul's letters.[4] This debate is reflected in the footnotes in the New Revised Standard Version: "the faith *of* Jesus Christ," not "faith *in* Jesus Christ" (Gal 2:16); "the faith *of* Jesus Christ," not "faith *in* Jesus Christ" (Rom 3:22; Gal 3:22); "the faith *of* Jesus," not "faith *in* Jesus" (Rom 3:26); "the faith *of* Christ," not "faith *in* Christ" (Gal 2:16; Phil 3:9); and "the faith *of* the Son of God," not "faith *in* the Son of God" (Gal 2:20). These footnotes indicate that New Testament scholars are debating a major item in Paul's theology— namely, how a person becomes justified.[5] Is it through [our] faith *in* Christ or through *Christ's* faith? We cannot be certain.

A Question of Grammar

The debate hinges upon the translation of a simple two-word Greek phrase: *pistis Christou*. *Pistis* can have two meanings:

1. belief, faith, trust, confidence
2. faithfulness, trustworthiness, reliability, fidelity, commitment

It is likely, however, that Paul's use of *pistis* carries *both* meanings, with sometimes one and sometimes the other predominating. To simplify matters, therefore, we can say that *pistis* means "faith/faithfulness." Paul says that people are justified through *faith/faithfulness.*

The second word in the Greek phrase, *Christou*, is the *genitive* form of the noun *Christos*, which, of course, is anglicized as "Christ." The genitive case can express various types of relationships. When a noun or pronoun in the genitive case modifies a noun (such as *pistis*) that involves some kind of physical, mental, volitional, or emotional *activity*, the genitive can be either an *ob-

jective genitive (the word in the genitive case is the *object* of the activity indicated by the noun it modifies) or a *subjective* genitive (the word in the genitive case is the *subject* of the activity indicated by the noun it modifies). Sometimes, however, it is unclear which is intended. For example, "the love of Christ" (2 Cor 5:14) can mean either "[our] love for Christ" (*objective* genitive) or "Christ's love [for us]" (*subjective* genitive), and "the love of God" (Rom 5:5) can mean either "God's love [for us]" (*subjective* genitive) or "[our] love for God" (*objective* genitive).

The question, then, is whether *Christou* in the phrase *pistis Christou* is an objective or a subjective genitive. If it is an *objective* genitive, then *pistis Christou* means "faith in/faithfulness to Christ"; if, however, *Christou* is a *subjective* genitive, then *pistis Christou* means "Christ's [own] faith/faithfulness." Grammatically, either interpretation is possible. Translators, therefore, need to look beyond the grammar of a given sentence for clues about the precise meaning of the phrase. In what follows, I shall summarize the reasoning for and against translating *pistis Christou* first as an objective genitive and then as a subjective genitive. Admittedly, this debate concerns a rather technical point of grammar, and so it might appear that scholars are making a great deal of fuss over such a small matter. The stakes, however, are high—both for our understanding of Paul and for Christian theology in the wake of the Reformation. If the *Christou* in *pistis Christou* is an objective genitive ("faith *in* Christ"), then Luther was right and Protestant theology since Luther has generally been on the right track so far as this issue is concerned. If, however, the *Christou* in *pistis Christou* is a subjective genitive ("the faith/faithfulness *of* Christ"), then Luther got it all wrong, and Protestant theology since Luther has generally been on the wrong track. Thus, the difference between "faith in/faithfulness to Christ" and "Christ's [own] faith/faithfulness" is important because it goes to the very heart of one of the major issues that sparked the Protestant Reformation.

Faith *in* (or Faithfulness *to*) Christ:
The Objective Genitive

Luther interpreted *Christou* as an objective genitive and translated *pistis Christou* into his native German as *Glauben an Christus* ("faith in Christ"). This became generally accepted, particularly by Protestants, and is still defended by many scholars. Various arguments have been advanced supporting the objective genitive interpretation:

1. Paul clearly does speak at times of "having faith in/being faithful to" Christ. For example, Philemon 5 refers to "the faith/faithfulness (*pistis*) that you have toward the Lord Jesus," and Paul twice employs the verb *pisteuein* (cognate of the noun *pistis*) followed by the preposition *eis* ("into" or "in") with "Christ Jesus" or its equivalent as the object of the preposition (Gal 2:16; Phil 1:29). Particularly significant is the usual understanding of Gal 2:16, which I here translate using "trust" for *pistis*:

   > But knowing that a person is not justified by works of law but by trust in Jesus Christ [*pistis Iēsou Christou*], we also have trusted in Christ Jesus [*eis Christon Iēsoun episteusamen*] in order that we might be justified by trust in Christ [*pistis Christou*] and not by works of law, because by works of law no one will be justified.

   Notice how the phrase with *eis* ("have trusted *in*") occurs between the two *pistis Christou* phrases. This arrangement within a single sentence can be taken as strong evidence that Paul intended all three phrases to carry the same meaning.

2. Paul frequently uses the verb *pisteuein* independently, without an object, to characterize the desired stance of his readers—that is, to refer to *human* faith/faithfulness.[6] Indeed, he regards *pistis* as a "fruit of the Spirit" (Gal 5:22). This suggests that the *pistis* Paul talks about is something that humans exercise, not something that Christ exhibits.

3. Paul appears to draw a parallel between the "faith/faithfulness" of Abraham and that of his readers (Gal 3:6–9; Rom 4:1–25). Again, this suggests that he is talking about the *pistis* that is exercised by humans, not by Christ.

4. Typically, when Paul employs the subjective genitive to indicate someone's "faith/faithfulness," he includes the definite article "the" before "faith/faithfulness,"[7] but the definite article *never* appears in the phrase *pistis Christou*.

This suggests that *Christou* in this phrase is not a subjective genitive.

5. There are similar phrases in which the genitive is clearly an *objective* genitive, including "the knowledge of Christ Jesus my Lord" (Phil 3:8) and "zeal for God" (Rom 10:2).

The force of these arguments is such that, *on strictly exegetical grounds* (that is, on the basis of a careful examination of individual passages), the *objective* genitive interpretation of *pistis Christou* (that is "faith in/faithfulness to Christ") might appear to be preferable.

Critics argue, however, that the objective genitive interpretation suggests a rather serious contradiction in Paul's theology. He says that people cannot be justified by "works of law"—that is, by things they *do* (or *don't do*),* but only by having faith in/being faithful to Christ. This, too, however, is something that people either *do* or *don't do*; people either *do* or *do not* exhibit faith in/faithfulness to Christ. Thus, justification by faith in/faithfulness to Christ suggests that people can *work* their way into a right relationship with God (that is, justification) by having faith in/being faithful to Christ. In principle, this would appear to be no different from *working* one's way into a right relationship with God by following the commandments—that is, by being good.

Some theologians have responded to this argument by maintaining that, for Paul, faith is a gift of God, not something that is self-generated. This, however, raises another serious theological problem: some people have faith and others do not. This suggests that God arbitrarily chooses to bestow the gift of faith on some but not on others. Although Paul occasionally suggests that such is the case (see, for example, Rom 8:29–30, which, however, may be a later interpolation, and Rom 9:10–18), the main thrust of his

---

*Some scholars now argue that "works of law" refers specifically to the ceremonial practices that distinguished Jews from Gentiles (for example, circumcision, the dietary laws, and Sabbath observance). I find this argument unconvincing, however, because Paul sometimes speaks of "works" without mentioning the Jewish Law. See, for example, Rom 4:4–5, which speaks of the "wage" to "the one who works" as something that is owed and the "wage" to "the one who does not work" as "grace."

message is that people can choose whether or not to be "reconciled to God" (Rom 5:20).

Faith or Faithfulness *of* Christ: The Subjective Genitive

In light of the above, and for other reasons as well, a few scholars have long argued, and more are now insisting, that the genitive in *pistis Christou* is a *subjective* genitive and that the phrase should therefore be translated as "Christ's faith/faithfulness."[8] Various arguments have been advanced supporting this interpretation.

1. The most literal translation of *pistis Christou* ("faith/faithfulness of Christ") would appear to support the subjective genitive interpretation.[9]
2. There are no instances in Paul's letters where a genitive with *pistis* must be understood as an objective genitive, but there are places where it must be understood as a subjective genitive. For example, Rom 1:8 refers to "your faith/faithfulness" (*hē pistis hēmōn*), and Rom 4:5, 4:12, and 4:16 refer, respectively, to "his [that is, Abraham's] faith/faithfulness" (*hē pistis autou*), "the faith/faithfulness of Abraham" (*hē pistis Abraam*) and "Abraham's faith/faithfulness" (*pistis Abraam*), employing what is clearly a subjective genitive for Abraham.[10] Moreover, Rom 3:3 refers to "the faithfulness of God" (*hē pistis tou Theou*), and the meaning clearly is "God's faithfulness," not "faithfulness to God."[11]
3. Translating *pistis Christou* as "Christ's faith/faithfulness" overcomes the apparent contradiction in Paul's theology, mentioned earlier, that is created by the objective genitive interpretation and would appear to be more in line with Paul's overall theological perspective, which stresses *God's* activity *in Christ* to effect human salvation.

If *pistis Christou* is translated as "Christ's faith/faithfulness," a clue to what Paul means by the phrase can be found in Rom 1:5, where he apparently equates *pistis* and *hypakoē* ("obedience").[12] This, in turn, points to Rom 5:18–19, where Paul contrasts Christ and Adam in the following words (New Revised Standard Version, emphasis mine):

Therefore just as one man's *trespass* led to condemnation for all, so one man's *act of righteousness* leads to justification and life for all. For just as by the one man's *disobedience* the many were made sinners, so by the one man's *obedience* the many will be made righteous.[13]

The contrast is between Adam's "trespass"/"disobedience," which establishes people as "sinners" and leads to "condemnation for all," and Christ's "act of righteousness"/"obedience," which establishes people as "righteous" (that is, "justified") and leads to "justification and life for all."* Christ's act of righteousness/obedience, *reverses* the trespass/disobedience of Adam. This obedience is then spelled out more explicitly in Phil 2:8, which says that Christ "became obedient to the point of death—even death on a cross." When Paul speaks, therefore, of "Christ's faith/faithfulness" as the basis for justification, he has in mind Christ's faithful obedience to the will of God, obedience that led to his death on the cross. In Paul's mind, it is Christ's faithful obedience, and this alone, that is the basis for justification.

There is, however, a problem here for modern interpreters of Paul. When Paul says that Christ's "obedience" reverses the "disobedience" of Adam, he clearly is assuming that Adam was an actual historical character and that the Genesis creation accounts are real *history*. These accounts, however, are not history; they are *myth*, and, as such, must be demythologized if they are to have meaning for those who understand the difference between myth and history. The biblical creation stories express profound truths about the human condition, including the fact that we experience ourselves as somehow alienated, separated from God, the Ground of Our Being. Thus, a demythologized interpretation of Paul's statement that Christ's obedience reverses Adam's disobedience might be something such as the following: our experience of alienation—of not being in a right relationship with God—is not the real and final truth about our relationship to God, the Ground of our Being. The real truth, as Paul puts it

---

*The words "righteousness," "justification," and "righteous" all come from the same root as the word translated in Gal 2:16 as "to be justified."

in 2 Cor 5:19, is that "God in Christ was *reconciling* the world unto himself" (emphasis mine)—in other words, that, whether we recognize it or not, we are *already* "reconciled" or "justified," rightly related to God, quite apart from anything we may do. Thus, Luther was on the right track when he denied that human "works" could lead to justification, but he should have gone further by also denying that human "faith/faithfulness" could lead to justification.

Conclusion

The debate between the objective genitive and subjective genitive interpretations of *pistis Christou* has not been resolved. Exegetical arguments might appear to support the *objective* genitive interpretation, while arguments based on Paul's overall theological perspective appear to support the *subjective* genitive interpretation. The evidence is rather evenly balanced, but, in my judgment, taken as a whole, it supports the *subjective* genitive interpretation: people are justified not by what they do ("works") but rather by Christ's faith/faithfulness.* In any case, the surprise is that we cannot be certain whether Paul bases "justification" on faith in/ faithfulness to Christ or on Christ's [own] faith/faithfulness. How one translates the phrase, however, is critically important for an understanding of Paul's theology.

Addendum

If Paul did in fact believe that people are justified by Christ's own faith/faithfulness, not by anything they themselves might do (including having faith in/being faithful to Christ), a crucially important theological question is raised: Does this mean that *all* people are (or ultimately will be) justified? In other words, does the logic of Paul's thought regarding justification lead him in the direction of *universalism*—that is, ultimate salvation for *everyone*? And does Paul himself move in this direction? This is the question that will be addressed in chapter 5.

*It is even possible that Paul did not draw the clear-cut distinction between *subjective* and *objective* genitive that modern grammarians insist upon and that he used the phrase with both possible meanings in mind, with one or the other coming to the forefront depending upon the particular point he is attempting to make.

Paul on Eschatology

The word "eschatology" comes from two Greek words: *eschatos* (which means "last," "final," or "ultimate") and *logos* (which means "word" or "speech"). Thus, "eschatology" means speech about "last things" or about what is sometimes called "the end time." Eschatological statements appear in the synoptic Gospels (Matthew, Mark, and Luke) on the lips of Jesus,[1] and it should come as no surprise to find eschatological materials in the letters of Paul.

The Surprise
- Paul's vision of the end time shifted to a more futuristic eschatology.

A close examination of these materials, however, leads to a surprising result: Paul's vision of the end time—his eschatology—apparently moves from what scholars call an *imminent* eschatology (Christ will return in the very near future) to a more *futuristic* eschatology (Paul himself may not be alive when Christ returns). In what is probably his earliest surviving letter, 1 Thessalonians, Paul is quite explicit about what he thinks will happen at the end time. First Thess 4:15–17 reads as follows in the New Revised Standard Version:

> For this we declare to you by the word of the Lord, that we who are alive, who are left until the coming of the Lord, will by no means precede those who have died. For the Lord himself, with a cry of command, with the archangel's call and with the sound of

God's trumpet, will descend from heaven, and the dead in Christ will rise first. Then we who are alive, who are left, will be caught up in the clouds together with them to meet the Lord in the air; and so we will be with the Lord forever.

Notice the repetition of the pronoun "we" in this passage—not "they" but "we." It is clear that Paul expects the Lord to return *while he and at least some of his readers are still alive.* A similar scenario appears in 1 Cor 15:51–52, which the New Revised Standard Version translates as follows:

Listen, I tell you a mystery! We will not all die, but we will all be changed, in a moment, in the twinkling of an eye, at the last trumpet. For the trumpet will sound, and the dead will be raised imperishable, and we will be changed.

Notice the contrast between "the dead" (those who have died) and the "we" (those who are still alive). "*The dead* will be raised imperishable," and "*we* will be changed." Here, as in 1 Thess 4:15–17, it is clear that Paul expects *at least some of his readers, and he himself as well,* to be alive when the Lord returns.

A rather different scenario appears, however, in 2 Cor 4:16–5:9,[2] which reads as follows in the New Revised Standard Version:

So we do not lose heart. Even though our outer nature is wasting away, our inner nature is being renewed day by day. For this slight momentary affliction is preparing us for an eternal weight of glory beyond all measure, because we look not at what can be seen but at what cannot be seen; for what can be seen is temporary, but what cannot be seen is eternal. For we know that if the earthly tent we live in is destroyed, we have a building from God, a house not made with hands, eternal in the heavens. For in this tent we groan, longing to be clothed with our heavenly dwelling—if indeed, when we have taken it off we will not be found naked. For while we are still in this tent, we groan under our burden, because we wish not to be unclothed but to be further clothed, so that what is mortal may be swallowed up by life. He who has prepared us for this very thing is God, who has given us the Spirit as a guarantee. So we are always confident; even though we know that while we are at home in the body we are away from the Lord—for we walk by faith, not by sight. Yes, we do have confidence, and we would rather be away from the body and at home with the Lord. So whether we are at home or away, we make it our aim to please him.

Here, Paul indicates that he is now "at home in the body" and thus "away from the Lord" but that he will die and then be "away from the body" and thus "at home with the Lord." There is nothing at all here about the *return* of the Lord. Rather, the imagery appears to be simply that of leaving the body, going to the heavenly dwelling, there to be "at home" with the Lord. Something appears to have changed in Paul's thinking about eschatology between the time he wrote 1 Thessalonians and 1 Corinthians and the time he wrote 2 Corinthians.

A somewhat similar idea appears in Phil 1:20–26, which also was almost certainly composed later than 1 Thessalonians and 1 Corinthians (it was written from prison, and it may, in fact, be the latest of Paul's surviving letters). The passage reads as follows in the New Revised Standard Version:

It is my eager expectation and hope that I will not be put to shame in any way, but that by speaking with all boldness, Christ will be exalted now as always, whether by life or by death. For to me, living is Christ and dying is gain. If I am to live in the flesh, that means fruitful labor for me; and I do not know which I prefer. I am hard pressed between the two: my desire is to depart and be with Christ, for that is far better; but to remain in the flesh is more necessary for you. Since I am convinced of this, I know that I will remain and continue with all of you for your progress and joy in faith, so that I may share abundantly in your boasting in Christ Jesus when I come to you again.

Here again, there is nothing about the return of the Lord. Rather there are simply the two options: remaining "in the flesh" or "depart[ing] and be[ing] with Christ."

Has Paul given up on the idea of the return of the Lord? This is unlikely, although it is the case that he has very little to say about it in the letters other than 1 Thessalonians and 1 Corinthians. What Paul apparently has given up, however, is the expectation that the Lord will return during his own lifetime. He is now facing the very real possibility and even probability that he will die before the Lord returns. In other words, he no longer expects the return of the Lord in the immediate future, as he apparently had expected it earlier on.

In short, the surprise is that Paul's vision of the end time—his eschatology—has apparently shifted from what scholars call an imminent eschatology to a more futuristic eschatology.

A Possible Reason for the Surprise

How do we account for this apparent change in Paul's eschatological expectation? Of course, it could be simply the passing of time and Paul's own realization that he was getting on in years, that he no longer enjoyed the vigor of youth, and that death—perhaps martyrdom—might not be far away. But the time span between 1 Thessalonians and 2 Corinthians was probably no more than five years or so. It's not as though a decade or more had passed. So, is there anything *in particular* that might have caused Paul to revise his earlier eschatological expectation?

We cannot be certain, but there may be a few hints in Paul's own letters (and I should note at this point that what I am about to suggest is certainly not original with me; it has been proposed by several scholars). In 1 Cor 15:32—a verse that is notoriously difficult both to translate and to interpret—Paul asks the question, "What do I gain if, humanly speaking, I fought with beasts at Ephesus?" We have no idea what this means. Does it mean that Paul was literally thrown into the arena to fight with wild animals? Some early Christian writings assumed this to be the case, but most modern scholars doubt it. At the very least, however, it does suggest that Paul faced some kind of difficult and perhaps even life-threatening situation in Ephesus.[3]

Then, in the opening chapter of 2 Corinthians (verses 3–7), Paul refers to his own "affliction" and "suffering" and goes on to write the following words (verses 8–10 as translated in the New Revised Standard Version):

> For we do not want you to be ignorant, brothers, of the afflic-
> tion we experienced in Asia [*note*: the major city in the Roman
> province of Asia was Ephesus]; for we were so utterly, unbearably
> crushed that we despaired of life itself. Why, we felt that we had
> received the sentence of death; but that was to make us rely not

on ourselves but on God who raises the dead; he delivered us from so deadly a peril, and he will deliver us; on him we have set our hope that he will deliver us again.

Apparently, something happened in Asia (Ephesus?) that caused Paul to think he was about to die. Confirmation of this may be found in Acts 19:23–41, which reports a riot in the city of Ephesus while Paul was there, and it is clear that what is pictured is a lynch mob that was aimed at Paul and his companions. According to the narrative, Paul was able to escape, and he left Ephesus and went to Greece.[4]

In short, Paul may speak in 1 Cor 15:32 of "fighting with beasts" in Ephesus, and he does refer in 2 Cor 1:3–10 to "affliction" and "suffering," indicating that, while he was in Asia (of which Ephesus was the major city), he "despaired of life itself." Then, Acts 19:32–41 tells of a lynch mob that wanted to kill Paul and his companions. In my judgment, it is possible that it was this experience, in Ephesus, that triggered the shift in Paul's eschatological thinking. Previously, he had simply assumed that he would still be living when the Lord returned. Now, perhaps for the first time, he was forced to face the very real possibility that he might die *before* the Lord returned.

Previously, Paul had assumed that Christians who died would be raised up when the Lord returned, but he had expected this to happen *very* soon—within his own lifetime. Then, the question was raised in Paul's mind: "What if it doesn't happen as soon as I thought it would? What if I die before the Lord comes? What will become of me?" And, more specifically, "Will I have to wait until the return of the Lord (whenever that may be) to be raised from the dead? Will there be a period of time during which I simply will not exist as a living person?" And Paul's answer now becomes, "No, I won't have to wait until the return of the Lord to be alive with the Lord. When I die, I will go immediately to be with the Lord. I won't have to wait until he returns to earth."

If this apparent shift in Paul's eschatology was indeed a response to his own existential situation, this means that his thinking was influenced by his experience and that he, like all of us, could change his mind, in light of that experience, about important items of faith. In any case, however, the surprise is that there does appear, in fact, to be a real shift in Paul's eschatological thinking between the time when he wrote 1 Thessalonians and 1 Corinthians and the time when he wrote 2 Corinthians and Philippians.

5

Paul on
Universal Salvation

In chapter 3, I discussed what may have been Paul's belief that people are *justified* (that is, brought into a right relationship with God) purely and simply on the basis of Christ's faith/faithfulness and not on the basis of anything at all that they themselves might do—in terms either of observable behavior or of inner attitudes or beliefs. This raises the question, does Paul believe that *everyone* either already has been or at some point will be justified—in other words, that *everyone* will ultimately be saved? Are the universalists right? Is Paul really a universalist? If he *is*, this will no doubt come as a surprise to most readers. I suggest, however, that the answer to the question of whether Paul is a universalist is rather more complicated than a simple yes or no and that, in order to answer the question, it really needs to be broken down into five parts.

1. Does Paul ever indicate that there are people who will not be saved? The answer to this question has to be yes. In several passages, Paul draws a clear distinction between those who are "being saved" and those who are "perishing" (for example, 1 Cor 1:18; 2 Cor 2:15–16; 4:3). In several places, Paul also warns of impending "wrath" that will befall certain people (for example, 1 Thess 1:10; 2:16; 5:9; Rom 1:18; 2:5, 8; 3:5; 4:15; 5:9; 9:22). And Paul speaks about the "destruction" of certain people (for example, Phil 3:18–19). Perhaps most graphic is 1 Thess 5:3, which reads, "When they say, 'There is peace and security,' then sudden destruction will come upon them, as labor pains come upon a pregnant woman, and there will be no escape."

47

This theme of judgment and destruction is particularly prevalent in 1 Thessalonians, which is probably the earliest of Paul's surviving letters. The perspective of 1 Thessalonians has been summarized by M. Eugene Boring as follows: "There are two, and only two, groups" among humankind: the *"we"* and the *"they."* On the one hand, *"we"* have been chosen (1:4); *"we"* have been delivered from the wrath to come (1:10); *"we"* live in hope (4:13); *"we"* shall be raised from the dead or caught up to meet the returning Lord in the air, to be with the Lord forever (4:16–17); *"we"* are not in the darkness, but are sons of the light and sons of the day (5:4–5); *"we"* belong to the day (5:8). *"They,"* on the other hand, do not have hope (4:13); *"they"* belong to the darkness (5:5–6); *"they"* will not be delivered from the wrath to come, and *their* fate will be destruction (5:3).[1] In short, according to this picture, some will be saved, and some will not.

This probably comes as no surprise to most of us. It is precisely what we would have expected from Paul. I note, however, that Paul says a lot more about those who *will* be saved than about those who *will not*, and this suggests that he is primarily interested in the former group.

2. Does Paul indicate who the people are who will not be saved? In some passages, it is clearly non-Christians who are in Paul's mind (for example, Phil 1:28; 3:18–19). The in group is the Christians, and the out group is the non-Christians. Thus, the answer to the question of who will *not* be saved appears to be that it is non-Christians.

But there are other passages that suggest a quite different answer. In 2 Cor 5:10, for example, Paul says, "For all of us must appear before the judgment seat of Christ, so that each may receive recompense for what has been done in the body, whether good or evil." This indicates that *everyone* will be judged—both Christians and non-Christians—that *everyone* will be either rewarded or punished—both Christians and non-Christians—and that the basis for the judgment will be what has been done in the body, that is to say, behavior. Along somewhat the same lines, Gal 5:19–21 says that the people who "will not inherit the kingdom of God" are those who are guilty of certain unacceptable forms of behavior, such as fornication, impurity, licentiousness, idolatry, sorcery, enmities, strife, jealousy, anger, quarrels, dissensions, factions, envy, drunkenness, and carousing. There is no mention here of whether these people are Christians or non-Christians. A somewhat similar list of vices appears in 1 Cor 6:9–10, with the warning that "none of these will inherit the kingdom of God." Again, the distinction is between those who are guilty of certain vices and those who are not—not between Christians and non-Christians. In these passages, Paul appears to be saying that the people who will not be saved are not necessarily non-Christians but rather the people whose lives are characterized by immoral and evil behavior.[2]

So, which is it? Is it non-Christians who will not be saved, or is it people whose conduct is judged unsatisfactory, regardless of whether they are Christian believers or non-Christians? Paul does not give a clear-cut answer to this question, and this, again, suggests that he is not particularly interested in the people who will *not* be saved.

3. Does Paul indicate what will ultimately become of the people who are not saved? Here, there may be something of a surprise, because Paul is remarkably vague at this point. The word "Hell"—"*Gehenna*"—never appears in the letters of Paul, nor does the word "Hades." Paul says nothing about "fire and brimstone" or about "weeping and wailing and gnashing of teeth."

To be sure, there is one passage in 2 Thessalonians (1:6–9) that describes in rather graphic detail the fate of the condemned, but 2 Thessalonians is regarded by a growing number of New Testament scholars (and I am one of them) as a pseudonymous writing (that is, written by someone other than Paul but attributed to him). Even in this passage, however, the picture is rather sparse: It speaks of "vengeance," "affliction," "separation from the presence of the Lord," and "eternal destruction," but there is nothing at all like what we find in Matt 13:42 and Matt 13:50, which speak of "the furnace of fire, where there will be weeping and gnashing of teeth," or like Mark 9:43, which refers to "the unquenchable fire," or like Matt 25:41, which speaks of "the eternal fire prepared for the devil and his angels," or like Rev 20:14–15, which refers to "the lake of fire." Second Thess 1:6–10 has simply "vengeance," "affliction," "separation from the presence of the Lord," "eternal destruction."

In short, even if we were to include 2 Thess 1:6–9, Paul would be remarkably vague regarding the fate of the unsaved. Although he divides humankind into two groups—the saved and the unsaved—and has a lot to say about the destiny of the saved, he says remarkably little about the fate of the unsaved, and most of what he does say is essentially negative: They will *not* be able to "escape the judgment of God" (Rom 2:3); they will *not* be "rescued" from "the wrath that is coming" (1 Thess 1:10; cf. 1 Thess 5:9; Rom 1:18; 2:5; 3:6); they will *not* be "caught up in the clouds . . . to meet the Lord in the air . . . and . . . be with the Lord forever" (1 Thess 4:17); they will *not* be able to "escape" the "sudden destruction [that] will come upon them, as labor pains come upon a pregnant women" (1 Thess 5:3; cf. Phil 1:28; 3:18–20); they will *not* "inherit the kingdom of God" (Gal 5:21; 1 Cor 6:9–11); they are in process of "perishing," even as Christians are in process of "being saved" (1 Cor 1:18; cf. 2 Cor 2:15; 4:3); they "deserve to die" (Rom 1:32) and in fact are destined for death (Rom 8:6); they are "condemned" (1 Cor 11:32); they are "still in [their] sins" (1 Cor 15:17), just as they are "imprisoned . . . under the power of sin" (Gal 3:22). But this is all rather vague, and it very well could mean little more than that the unsaved will simply be destroyed—that death will be the end of their existence. There is nothing explicitly about eternal punishment or eternal torment. In short, Paul is remarkably vague about what will become of the people who are not saved, and this, again, suggests that he is not particularly interested in them.

4. Why does Paul even talk about the people who will not be saved? The fact that Paul appears to be both ambiguous regarding the identity of the people who will not be saved and vague regarding their destiny suggests that Paul is not particularly interested in what I have called the out group. This raises a question, though: Why does he bother to say anything at all about these people? Why not simply disregard or ignore them? It could be, of course, that Paul refers to these people as a warning to his readers—to ensure that they not be a part of this group. But

Boring, to whom I have already referred, thinks there may be a different reason. He suggests that what Paul says about the fate of the unsaved is intended simply as a foil for what he really wants to say about the saved. To say it a bit differently, Paul is playing what the German philosopher Ludwig Wittgenstein would call a particular "language game," and the game itself requires him to say something about the unsaved. You can't hold the notion of being saved without somehow holding the opposite notion of not being saved or being lost. It's something like win and lose: you can't talk about winning without at least implying something about losing. According to this view, Paul is not really interested in talking about those who are unsaved, but he has to at least give some intimation of what it means to be unsaved if being saved is to have any meaning. You can't really understand what it means to win unless you have some understanding of what it means to lose, just as you can't really understand the meaning of good unless you have some understanding of the meaning of evil. Thus, according to Boring, at least much of what Paul has to say about the unsaved is intended simply by way of contrast, to help people understand what it means to be saved. This leads inevitably, however, to the notion of a group of insiders, recipients of the gracious action of God, and the contrasting notion of a group of outsiders, who are not recipients of the grace of God. It also leads inevitably to a picture of judgment, of separation, of sorting out—some on the right hand and some on the left, some who receive a positive judgment and some who receive a negative judgment.[3]

In short, when Paul plays this particular "language game," he is pretty well compelled to separate the human race into two groups: the in group and the out group, the saved and the unsaved. And this is precisely what Paul does in the passages that we have looked at. But this is by no means the end of the matter, because another group of texts in Paul's letters appears to give a quite different picture—a picture that perhaps comes as a real surprise.

5. Is it possible that everyone ultimately will be saved? In Rom 11:26, Paul says that "*all* Israel will be saved," and he goes on to suggest, in verses 28 and 29, that this will be not because they have faith in Christ or because of anything they have done but rather because of God's election and calling, because of God's covenant

with them. Then, in verse 32, Paul goes even further: He says that "God has imprisoned *all* in disobedience so that he may be merciful to *all*." And the preceding verses make it clear that Paul is now talking about both Jews and Gentiles. *All* were imprisoned in disobedience, but God will be merciful to *all*—not because of anything they have done but simply because of God's mercy.

Other passages point in the same direction. Second Cor 5:19 says that "in Christ God was reconciling *the world* to himself, not counting their trespasses against them"—reconciling not just part of the world, but "the world." Phil 2:6–11 says that God has "highly exalted" Jesus and given him "the name that is above every name, so that at the name of Jesus *every knee* should bend, in heaven and on earth, and under the earth, and *every tongue* should confess that Jesus Christ is Lord to the glory of God the Father." Not *some* knees and *some* tongues, but *every* knee and *every* tongue. To be sure, some people have read this to mean that ultimately everyone will confess Jesus as Lord but that some will do so gladly and joyfully and others only grudgingly and under coercion, but there is nothing in the text itself to suggest this interpretation. It simply says that *everyone* will confess Jesus as Lord.

Furthermore, 1 Cor 15:22 says: "For as *all* die in Adam, so *all* will be made alive in Christ." Although some scholars have interpreted this to mean that "all who are in Adam" die and "all who are in Christ" will be made alive, this is not the most natural reading of the text. A literal translation of the text reads, "For as in Adam all die, so also in Christ all will be made alive." *All* die in Adam, and *all* are "made alive in Christ"—not *some* but *all*.

Most striking are some verses in the fifth chapter of Romans. In verse 12, Paul says "that sin came into the world through one man [Adam], and death spread to *all* because *all* have sinned." But then, in verses 15–21, he says (Revised Standard Version, emphasis added):

> But the free gift is not like the trespass. For if the *many* died through one man's trespass, much more surely have the grace of God and the free gift in the grace of the one man, Jesus Christ, abounded for the *many*. And the free gift is not like the effect of the one man's sin. For the judgment following one trespass brought condemnation, but the free gift following many tres-

passes brings justification. If, because of the one man's trespass, death exercised dominion through that one, much more surely will those who receive the abundance of grace and the free gift of righteousness exercise dominion in life through the one man, Jesus Christ. Therefore just as one man's trespass led to condemnation for *all*, so one man's act of righteousness leads to justification and life for *all*. For just as by the one man's disobedience the *many* were made sinners, so by the one man's obedience the *many* will be made righteous. But law came in, with the result that the trespass multiplied; but where sin increased, grace abounded all the more, so that, just as sin exercised dominion in death, so grace might also exercise dominion through justification leading to eternal life through Jesus Christ our Lord.

To be sure, there is an alternation in this passage between "many" and "all," but it is clear that "many" is to be interpreted in light of "all," not *vice versa*, and that what Paul really means is "all." Certainly, when Paul is talking about Adam, "many" means "all." In verse 15, Paul says that *many* died through one man's trespass, but in verse 12 he has already said that death spread to *all*. So, the "many" in verse 15 is to be interpreted in light of the "all" in verse 12. "Many" really means "all." Paul is saying simply that, because of Adam's transgression, *all* sinned and, as a result, *all* died. Similarly, in verse 19, Paul says that *many* were made sinners by one man's disobedience, but in verse 18 he has already said that one man's trespass led to condemnation for *all*. So, here again, "many" really means "all."

Thus, with reference to Adam, "many" clearly means "all," and the parallelism between Adam and Christ in the passage suggests the same with reference to Christ. In verse 15, Paul says that God's free gift of grace abounded for the *many*, and in verse 19 he says that by one man's obedience the *many* will be made righteous, but in verse 18 he says that one man's act of righteousness leads to justification and life for *all*. Here again, "many" really means "all."

In addition, Paul insists several times in this passage that what happens in Christ is "much more" than what happened in Adam: "If the many died through one man's trespass," *much more* has God's grace "abounded for the many" (verse 15); "where sin increased, grace abounded *much more*" (verse 20), and the Greek here reads literally, "where sin increased, grace super-abounded." Now, if Adam's sin affects *all* people, but Christ's righteousness affects only *some* people, it would be difficult to see how grace abounds *even more* than sin. In short, Paul appears to be saying in Rom 5:12–21 that just as *all* people were brought under the power of sin through Adam's transgression, so *all* people will be freed from the power of sin through Christ's righteousness—in other words, that *all* people will ultimately be brought into a right relationship with God.

Conclusion

Well, there you have it: one set of passages where Paul divides people into two groups: the in group and the out group, those who are saved and those who are not; and another set of passages where Paul appears to say that *all* people are ultimately to be brought into a right relationship with God. How is this apparent contradiction to be resolved, or at least explained? Some scholars have concluded that Paul was simply confused on the issue—that he had no clear or coherent position on the matter. And I suppose this is certainly possible. Others have insisted, however, that the contradiction is only apparent and that Paul did in fact have a clear and consistent position. Here, the apparent contradiction is resolved by subordinating one set of passages to the other: either the universalistic passages express Paul's *real* view and the particularistic passages are to be interpreted in their light, or *vice versa*.

Boring, however, whom I have already cited several times, takes a different approach. He suggests that Paul's Jewish heritage has provided him with more than one image of God and that the different images of God point to different conclusions regarding whether *all* people ultimately will be saved. There is the image of God as "the-God-who-elects"—the God who chooses one particular group of people to be his own people. According to this image, there is a clear distinction between the elect and the non-elect—for example, between Israel and "the nations" or between "the church" and "the world." And then there is the image of God as "the-God-who-judges"—the God who expects a certain standard of behavior and who rewards or punishes people in terms of how well they live up to this standard. Thus, when Paul divides people into the in group and the out group—those who are saved and those who are not, he is speaking from the perspective of the image of God as "the God-who-elects" or "the God-who judges." In terms of the God-who-elects, people are either chosen or not chosen; in terms of the God-who-judges, people either measure up to the required standard or they don't. Thus, in either case, you have the in group and the out group.

But Paul also has another image of God—and this image also comes to him from his Jewish heritage. This is the image of God as "the God-who-rules." And the pertinent question for the God-who-rules is, who is in charge? Is it God, or is it someone or something else? Thus, according to Boring, when Paul speaks in terms of universal salvation, he is speaking from the perspective of the image of God as the God-who-rules, the God who will ultimately triumph, the God whose purposes will finally be accomplished. And, according to this view, it is the will and purpose of God that none should perish but that all should be saved.[4]

I find Boring's suggestions most interesting and enlightening, but I would prefer to say it a little differently. I would prefer to say that Paul is committed to two images of God—each a part of his Jewish heritage. One is the image of God as the God of justice, and the other is the image of God as the God of grace. On the one hand, justice requires that hard decisions be made, that people endure the consequences of their own actions, that a distinction be made between the in group and the out group. Grace, on the other hand, without in any way denying the seriousness or the devastating consequences of human behavior, somehow transforms the human situation in such a way that every single person can ultimately have a place in the Kingdom of God.

It appears to me that the passages we have looked at reflect one or the other of these two images of God—either the God of justice or the God of grace. And it also appears to me that these two images of God struggled for predominance in Paul's own thinking. I think we find the first image—the God of justice—predominating in Paul's earlier letters: 1 Thessalonians, which is almost certainly the earliest, and, in a somewhat different way, in Galatians, which may be the next earliest. But the second image of God—the God of grace—is already present in the earlier letters, and it becomes more pronounced in 1 Corinthians, 2 Corinthians and Philippians, and receives its fullest expression in Romans, which I believe to be the latest of Paul's extant letters.

In short, it is my suggestion that the thinking of Paul was clearly moving in the direction of universalism when he wrote his letter to the Romans. I don't think he got all the way there—at least not in the letters that we have, but I think he was moving in this direction.

Why was his thinking moving in the direction of universalism? We can't be certain, of course, but my own hunch is that it was, at least in part, because he was increasingly recognizing the real implications of his conviction that people are brought into a right relationship with God not on the basis of anything they can do—whether this be being good or whether it be having faith in Christ—but purely and simply on the basis of Christ's faith/faithfulness—Christ's obedience to the will of God.

Is it accurate to call Paul a universalist? No, because he never got all the way there, at least in his letters that have survived. Is it appropriate to use materials in Paul's letters as an argument *for* universalism? My own judgment is that it is appropriate.

Paul on Women[1]

Thirteen of the twenty-seven books that make up the New Testament are letters attributed to Paul. Six of these thirteen letters contain passages that reflect a quite negative view of the character and capabilities of women and/or relegate women to a subordinate status and role: subordinate in the family, in the church, and, at least by implication, in society at large.[2]

In one of these passages (2 Tim 3:6–7), women are characterized as "silly," "overwhelmed by their sins," "swayed by all kinds of desires," and unable "to arrive at a knowledge of the truth" even when instructed. In another (1 Tim 5:13), young widows—that is, women not under the supervision of a husband or a male relative—are described as "idle," "gadding about from house to house," "gossips," "busybodies, saying what they should not"—behavior that gives "the adversary" an "occasion to revile us." Still another passage (1 Tim 2:13–14) declares that "Adam was not deceived, but the woman was deceived and became a transgressor."

Hand-in-hand with this negative portrayal of the character and capabilities of women go commands relegating them to a subordinate status and role in the family. Women are "to love their husbands, to love their children, to be self-controlled, chaste, good managers of the household, kind, being submissive to their husbands" (Titus 2:4–5). They are to "be subject" to their husbands just as slaves are to "be subject" to their masters and children to their parents (Eph 5:21–6:19; Col 3:18–4:1). A woman will be saved "through childbearing," but only if "they [presumably the children] continue in faith and love and holiness, with modesty" (1 Tim 2:15).

In the church, women are "to keep silent"; they are not permitted "to teach or to have authority over a man," and "if there is anything they desire to know," they are to "ask their husbands at home" (1 Tim 2:11–12; 1 Cor 14:34–35). When they do "pray" or "prophesy," they are to indicate their subordinate status by doing so with their heads covered (1 Cor 11:4–15). Women are to "dress themselves modestly and decently in suitable clothing, not with their hair braided, or with gold, pearls, or expensive clothes, but with good works, as is proper for women who profess reverence for God" (1 Tim 2:9–10).

This subordination of women reflects an ontological hierarchy in which "the husband is the head of his wife" just as "Christ is the head of every man" and "God is the head of Christ" (1 Cor 11:3). Moreover, this hierarchy is rooted in creation itself: "Adam was formed first, then Eve" (1 Tim 2:13) or, more specifically, whereas "man is the image and reflection of God," "woman is the reflection of man," and "man was not made from woman, but woman from man," and man was not "created for the sake of woman, but woman for the sake of man" (1 Cor 11:4–9). In short, "the husband is the head of the wife just as Christ is the head of the church" (Eph 5:23).

To be sure, within the passages just cited there are a few qualifications that appear to somewhat soften or mitigate their initial impact: Husbands are to love their wives and not "treat them harshly" (Col 3:19; see also Eph 5:25); indeed, "husbands should love their wives as they do their own bodies," for the two have "become one flesh" (Eph 5:25–33). Moreover, "in the Lord woman is not independent of man or man independent of woman, for just as woman came from man, so man comes through woman" (1 Cor 11:11–12). Nevertheless, the controlling presupposition even of these qualifications is that of a patriarchal society in which women are expected to be married, to have children, to be obedient and submissive wives and loving mothers, and, above all, to play no role of leadership in domestic, religious, or public affairs.

In light of such statements, George Bernard Shaw's characterization of Paul as "the eternal enemy of Woman" would surely appear to be correct.[3] It is my intention, however, to argue that Shaw was wrong—as have been most of Paul's interpreters, both defenders and detractors—and that the Apostle was, in fact, a "radical egalitarian" so far as the status and role of women are concerned. The basis for my argument will be four points, to which I now turn.

Egalitarian References to Particular Women

In addition to the passages already noted, there are other passages in Paul's letters that suggest a quite different attitude toward women. I have in mind certain more-or-less incidental and passing references to particular women—women with whom Paul was associated in his evangelistic and pastoral activities. Paul speaks, for example, of five different women—Euodia, Syntyche, Tryphaena, Tryphosa, and Mary—as his "fellow workers" or as "workers in the Lord" who have "worked hard" or "labored side by side" with him in various of the churches (Phil 4:2–3; Rom 16:6, 12). The terminology here is exactly the same as that which Paul uses elsewhere to characterize male associates who clearly are regarded as leaders in the churches (see 1 Thess 3:2; 1 Cor 3:9; 2 Cor 8:23; Phil 2:25; Phlm 1, 24; Rom 16:9–21). Furthermore, Paul praises a wife and husband, Prisca and Aquila, as his "fellow workers in Christ Jesus, who risked their necks" for him and in whose home a community of Jesus' followers meets for worship (1 Cor 16:19; Rom 16:3–5). The fact that Prisca is named first in Rom 16:3 and Aquila first in 1 Cor 16:19 suggests that Paul regards the two as of equal status and importance. In none of these incidental references to particular women does Paul in any way suggest that men and women play different roles or perform different functions or that the women are or should be in any way subordinate or subservient to the men.

Beyond this, Paul identifies a certain Phoebe as a "deacon [or minister] of the church at Cenchreae" (Rom 16:1), a title that he elsewhere applies generally to leaders in the church (Phil 1:1), including himself (1 Cor 3:5; 2 Cor 3:6; 6:4; 11:23).[4] In addition, he refers to her in the following verse as *prostatis*, which likely indicates a position of leadership and/or authority (not a "helper" as in the Revised Standard Version or a "benefactor" as in the

New Revised Standard Version). Even more striking is the fact that Paul refers in Rom 16:7 to his "fellow prisoners" Andronicus (a man) and Junia (a woman) not just as "apostles" but as "prominent among the apostles."* "Apostle" is, of course, Paul's title for a divinely appointed and officially authorized representative of and spokesperson for the church, and it is also the title most proudly and insistently claimed by Paul for himself (see especially 1 Cor 9:1–2 and Gal 1:1). In short, Paul recognizes women as both deacons and apostles.

Thus, in his incidental and passing references to particular women in the churches, Paul betrays none of the male-chauvinistic attitude so characteristic of the passages noted earlier. Quite to the contrary, he speaks of women as respected and equal partners, co-workers, and leaders in the churches. In these references, therefore, we have one clear line of evidence suggesting a much more egalitarian attitude and practice on the part of the Apostle than is generally assumed.

Egalitarian Views on Sex, Marriage, and Divorce

Until recently, chapter 7 of 1 Corinthians has almost universally been understood as an argument against marriage and, at least by implication, as a denigration of women. New Testament scholars, however, are now increasingly seeing the chapter as a ringing affirmation of complete equality within the marriage relation and of the right of both women and men to refrain from marriage if they so choose.

The principal concern of the chapter is whether sexual relations have any place in the Christian life. Apparently, some in the Corinthian church regarded the body and all bodily functions and activities as inherently evil—or at least "unspiritual"—and, for this reason, opposed sexual activity both within and outside the marriage relation. It appears that their slogan, as quoted by

---

*Most translators and commentators had long assumed that the name was "Junias" and that it designated a man (see, for example, the Revised Standard Version); recent studies have indicated, however, that the name almost certainly is "Junia" and that it designates a woman (as the New Revised Standard Version correctly recognizes). See, e.g., Epp, *Junia*. The nominative form of the accusative *Junian* could be either *Junias* (masculine) or *Junia* (feminine).

Paul at the beginning of the chapter, was, "It is well for a man not to touch a woman" (1 Cor 7:1b). There may have been others in the church, however, who regarded the body and bodily functions and activities as essentially irrelevant so far as true spirituality was concerned and thus allowed or perhaps even encouraged sexual activity not only within the marriage relation but also without benefit of marriage.

A careful reading of the chapter in its entirety indicates that Paul, in his response to these views, does essentially three things: (1) He suggests that most Christians should marry and should view sexual relations as an integral and vital part of the marriage relation (1 Cor 7: 2, 3, 5). (2) He insists that husbands and wives have precisely the same rights and responsibilities within the marriage relation—that is, that the marriage relation is one of complete mutuality and equality (1 Cor 7:2–4, 10–16). (3) Perhaps most significantly of all, he encourages those women and men who so desire to remain unmarried (1 Cor 7:8), not because marriage and sexuality are in any way sinful but rather because of the nearness of the end and for the sake of their "undivided devotion to the Lord" (1 Cor 7:29–35).

This last point was truly revolutionary, for it represented a radical break with the most basic of all patriarchal institutions, the patriarchal family. Women were expected to marry and have children. Paul insists, however, that both women and men may quite legitimately choose to remain single. Later, the unmarried state was apparently embraced by some Christian women who saw it as a way of escape from the oppressive state of marriage. This was increasingly opposed, however, by much of the male leadership of the church, who viewed the unmarried state as an occasion for instability and disorder within the church and criticism from outsiders (see, for example, 1 Tim 5:9–16).[5]

According to Paul, women and men are free either to marry or not to marry. If they do marry, theirs are to be marriages of mutual and equal privilege and mutual and equal responsibility. If they remain unmarried, they are in no way inferior or degraded; quite to the contrary, Paul positively desires such a state for all who are so inclined. In either case, women have the same privileges and responsibilities as do men.

If understood in this way, 1 Corinthians 7 is totally consistent with the egalitarianism indicated in Paul's incidental and passing references to particular women but is radically inconsistent with the patriarchal attitude of the passages cited earlier. Thus, we now have a second line of evidence suggesting a more egalitarian attitude and practice on the part of Paul than is generally assumed.

Egalitarian Baptismal Formula

In one particular passage, Paul quite clearly and unequivocally affirms his radically egalitarian position. The passage is Gal 3:27–28, which reads as follows in the New Revised Standard Version:

> For as many of you as were baptized into Christ have clothed yourselves with Christ. There is no longer Jew or Greek, there is no longer slave or free, there is no longer male and female; for all of you are one in Christ Jesus.

To be sure, this passage may well have been not Paul's own composition but rather a quotation from a pre-Pauline baptismal formula. By quoting it in his letter to the Galatians, however, Paul indicates his own conviction that, in Christ, all former distinctions of ethnicity, socio-economic status, and gender have been totally abolished.[6] This, of course, is quite consistent with the egalitarianism seen in Paul's references to particular women and in 1 Corinthians 7—indeed, it provides a theological rationale for such egalitarianism. Clearly, however, it flies in the face of the patriarchalism of the passages cited earlier. Thus, it would appear that we now have a third line of evidence suggesting a more egalitarian attitude and practice on the part of Paul than is generally assumed.

Before leaving Gal 3:27–28, however, it is necessary to consider a possible problem. In 1 Cor 12:13, Paul cites a baptismal formula quite similar to the one quoted in Gal 3:27–28 except that it omits the male-female pair: "For in the one Spirit we were all baptized into one body—Jews or Greeks, slaves or free—and we were all made to drink of one Spirit."[7] This omission is troubling because it might suggest that Paul is less than totally consistent, or even that he is somewhat ambivalent, in his egalitarianism regarding men and women. Various attempts have been made to explain the omission, but none of them is really satisfying. It is possible that Paul omits the male-female pair to avoid calling attention again to a major issue dividing the Corinthian church—the nature of human sexuality—that he has already dealt with earlier in the letter (1 Cor 5:1–5; 6:15–20; 7). It is also possible that the Galatian churches were familiar with one form of the baptismal formula and the church in Corinth with a different form and that Paul, in each case, simply uses the form with which his audience is familiar. In any case, however, the omission of male-female in 1 Cor 12:13 in no way cancels out its inclusion in Gal 3:27–28. Moreover, Gal 3:27–28, unlike 1 Cor 12:13, is consistent with the egalitarianism of Paul's incidental references to particular women and his egalitarian treatment of sex, marriage, and divorce; thus, in my judgment, it should carry greater weight in determining Paul's actual views regarding male-female relations. In short, despite the omission of male-female in 1 Cor 12:13, Paul's egalitarianism is clearly evidenced in Gal 3:27–28.

And now, before proceeding to the fourth point, it is appropriate to pause for an observation. If the baptismal formula in Gal 3:27–28, the discussion of sexuality and marriage in 1 Corinthians 7, and Paul's incidental references to particular women were all we had, we could easily conclude that Paul was indeed a radical egalitarian, and the matter would be closed. Unfortunately, however, things are not so simple. There still remain the passages cited earlier—passages that so clearly and unequivocally insist on male dominance and female subordination. What about these passages? And this question leads to the fourth point.

Non-Pauline Authorship of Patriarchal Passages

Briefly stated, the fourth point is this: none of the passages depicting women in a negative light and/or calling for male dominance and female subordination comes from Paul. All of them were written by people other than Paul, after the lifetime of Paul. Moreover, they most likely represent intentional and deliberate reactions against the radical egalitarianism of the Apostle. They come from the late first and early second centuries, when the expanding church was striving for some measure of peace, stability, and acceptance within Hellenistic-Roman society, which was, for the most part, overwhelmingly patriarchal in its basic attitudes and structures. Paul's radical egalitarianism was now increasingly seen as a threat, as were certain other aspects of his thought and practice, and it became necessary, at least in the minds of some, to "domesticate" the Apostle. In the first generations after Paul, there appear to have been at least three distinct ways of attempting this domestication.

The "Biographical" or "Romantic Novel"

One way of domesticating Paul was by composing what we might call "biographical" or "romantic novels"—narratives about Paul that present him in a less radical, more acceptable light. The New Testament contains one example of such a novel, The Acts of the Apostles, and there are others, including, for example, the second-century *Acts of Paul*. Apparently, one of the principal concerns in the canonical Acts of the Apostles is to bring Paul into the mainstream of the emerging "orthodox" consensus by playing down the more controversial and radical aspects of his theology and portraying him as subordinate to and in harmony with the Jerusalem leadership of the church. This portrayal reflected, among other things, what can only be seen as an "anti-feminine bias."[8] Thus, the radical egalitarianism that appears in points one, two, and three above becomes considerably muted in the book of Acts, where, for the most part, the important characters are all men.

Pseudonymity

A second way of "domesticating" Paul was the way of "pseudonymity"—writing new letters in the name of the Apostle.[9] Most New Testament scholars have long agreed that the "Pastoral Letters"—1 Timothy, 2 Timothy, and Titus—were not, in fact, written by Paul or even during Paul's lifetime. This conclusion is based on considerations quite unrelated to the question of women—considerations of vocabulary, literary style, ideational content, and implied historical provenance. It is precisely in these letters, however, that the most adamant and uncompromising support for patriarchal attitudes and practices appears. A somewhat smaller majority of scholars also agrees that Ephesians and

Colossians were not written by Paul or during his lifetime. Again, the crucial considerations are those of vocabulary, style, ideational content, and historical provenance, not the question of women. These letters also contain statements supporting male dominance and female subordination, although the statements here are somewhat less strident than those in the Pastoral Letters.

Both in the Pastorals and in Ephesians and Colossians, there appears a particular literary genre not found in any of the other letters attributed to Paul—the so-called "household code."[10] Here, the mutual relations and responsibilities of members of the household are spelled out—master and slave, parent and child, husband and wife. In each case, the latter is to be subservient to the former: slave to master, child to parent, and wife to husband. The genre is a common one in the Hellenistic world of the first and second centuries,[11] and it eventually found its way into the literature of the Christian movement. Earlier, however, in Paul's quotation of the baptismal formula in Gal 3:27–28, we see a clear rejection of both the master-slave and the male-female distinctions that figure so prominently in the household codes.

In short, it appears that after Paul's death letters were written in his name, the purpose of which, among other things, was to counter the radically egalitarian principles and practices advocated by Paul and apparently followed in at least some of his churches. These letters—the Pastorals, Ephesians, and Colossians—cannot, therefore, be used as sources for the reconstruction of Paul's own views. Only the letters actually written (or dictated) by Paul may be used for this purpose, and there are only two passages in these letters that support male dominance and female subordination. Both of these passages are in 1 Corinthians, and both of them are remarkably akin in vocabulary, style, and content to the passages noted in the pseudo-Pauline letters. And this leads to the third way in which attempts were made to domesticate Paul after his death.

Interpolation[12]

The third way of domesticating Paul was "interpolation," the addition of non-Pauline materials to the genuine letters of Paul. Despite continuing debate regarding details, there is now a widespread consensus among New Testament scholars that Paul's letters have not come down to us exactly as he wrote (or dictated) them. For example, it is now generally thought that what we know as 2 Corinthians is made up of parts of at least two or as many as five originally separate letters, and Philippians may contain parts of as many as three separate letters. The Pauline letters were subject to various types of editorial activity, and most scholars would agree, at least in principle, that this editorial activity likely included interpolation. It is difficult, of course, to identify interpolations with any degree of certitude, in part because of the ever-present danger of circular reasoning, in which certain presuppositions regarding Pauline vocabulary, style, and thought are used as evidence against Pauline authorship. There are, however, certain criteria that, in their cumulative effect, can sometimes indicate the probability of interpolation. These criteria include variations among manuscript readings,* the awkward fit of a passage in its present context, and apparently non-Pauline vocabulary, style, and/or ideational content.

It is now fairly widely agreed, even among some very conservative scholars, that one of the two Corinthian passages advocating male dominance and female subordination—1 Cor 14:34–35—is a non-Pauline interpolation.[13] I have argued, and a few other scholars have agreed, that the other such passage—1 Cor 11:3–16—is also an interpolation.[14] My argument is based primarily on the following considerations: (a) the passage appears to interrupt the context in which it appears, (b) it contains apparently non-Pauline vocabulary and style, (c) some of the content of the passage is difficult if not impossible to reconcile with Paul's thought as expressed elsewhere, and (d) there are some rather striking similarities between the passage and materials in the pseudo-Pauline writings. If, then, 1 Cor 14:34–35 and

---

*A passage may appear at different places in the various manuscripts. For example, 1 Cor 14:34–35 appears after verse 40 in a few manuscripts; and Rom 16:25–27 appears after 14:23 in some manuscripts, after Rom 15:33 in one of the oldest manuscripts, and at two or three different places in a few manuscripts. In addition, there are sometimes minor differences among the manuscripts immediately before and/or immediately after a passage suggesting various attempts to smooth the transition.

1 Cor 11:3–16 are in fact non-Pauline interpolations—and I am convinced that they are—then there is not a single statement from Paul himself that advocates or even suggests male dominance or female subordination. Rather, what we now have is a fourth line of evidence that is consistent with indications of Paul's radical egalitarianism, both in principle and in practice, as regards relations between women and men—an egalitarianism so radical that later writers and editors deemed it necessary to domesticate his message and influence.

Summary and Conclusion

On the basis of the four points just discussed, I conclude that it was not Paul who imposed the yoke of inequality and subservience on the women of the emerging Christian movement but rather later *Paulinists* who wrote letters in his name and/or added materials to his own letters. As history shows, it was also their views, not those of the Apostle, that triumphed—at least until recent times. Paul himself, however, is best understood in light of the baptismal formula of Gal 3:27–28:

> For as many of you as were baptized into Christ have clothed yourselves with Christ. There is no longer Jew or Greek, there is no longer slave or free, there is no longer male and female; for all of you are one in Christ Jesus.

Epilogue

My conclusion raises two important and interrelated questions: (1) *Why* was Paul so radically egalitarian in his attitude toward the status and role of women? (2) Was he *the first* to espouse and practice such egalitarianism, or was he building on some precedent that had already been established?

As regards the second question, I strongly suspect that women were in fact already playing roles of leadership in some of the churches before Paul came on the scene. I base this on four considerations: (1) It is clear that women played leading roles in some of the Hellenistic mystery religions of the time; thus, the idea of women as religious leaders would by no means have been completely new or strange to gentile members of the Jesus communities. (2) There is evidence that women also played roles of leadership in some Jewish synagogues;[15] thus, Jewish members of the Jesus communities may also have had knowledge and perhaps even experience of such leadership. (3) The gospels indicate that Jesus not only included women among his followers[16] but also apparently called into question the traditional patriarchal family structure.[17] (4) As has already been indicated, Gal 3:27–28—"there is no longer Jew or Greek, there is no longer slave or free, there is no longer male and female"—is widely regarded as a pre-Pauline baptismal formula, in which case Paul was by no means the first in the Jesus movement to articulate a radical egalitarianism regarding the status and role of women.[18] In short, Paul's views, while clearly radical within the first-century Greco-Roman world, would not have been unique or without precedent.

As regards the first question, perhaps Paul's egalitarian views were initially sparked, at least in part, by his encounters with women who were already leaders in some of the churches. In any case, however, it appears that by the time he wrote (or dictated) his letters, he not only *accepted* such egalitarianism but also sincerely and wholeheartedly *endorsed* and *celebrated* it.

Paul
on Sex[1]

A popular view of Paul is that he was opposed to sex. In an article entitled "Saint Paul Hated Sex," for example, Stephen A Patterson has recently asserted that Paul (a) regarded sex as "just raw passion" that one "ought to be able to resist," (b) saw those who were unable to resist it (and that meant most of us) as "spiritual sissies," and (c) reluctantly condoned marriage—and thus sex—only because "it is better to marry"—and presumably to engage in sexual relations with one's spouse—"than to be aflame with passion."[2]

I concede that Paul's attitude toward sex falls far short of our modern understanding of its positive value in the enrichment and enjoyment of human life, but, in this regard, he is no different from many of his contemporaries. I also acknowledge that, *in one passage* (1 Corinthians 7), Paul states a preference for celibacy over marriage and speaks of marriage as a safeguard against *porneia*—a Greek word that, for him, would refer to any sexual activity outside of marriage,[3] including, at least by implication, what is known today as homosexual activity.[4] Nevertheless, it is my judgment that the evidence regarding Paul's attitude toward sex is considerably more complex and nuanced than many suggest and by no means indicates unambiguously that Paul *hated* sex. What Paul *hated* was not sex *per se* but rather *porneia*.

As I have already indicated (see note 3), there are passages in 1 Corinthians, 2 Corinthians, and Galatians that indicate Paul's "hatred" of *porneia* (that is, sex *outside of marriage*), but it is only in 1 Corinthians, Romans, and perhaps 1 Thessalonians that we find evidence regarding Paul's attitude toward sex *within the marriage relationship.** At least five and perhaps six passages in these letters are relevant to any discussion of Paul's attitude toward sex.

1 Thessalonians 4:3–8

A passage in 1 Thessalonians (probably the earliest of Paul's extant letters), *may* indicate something regarding Paul's attitude toward sex. The passage is 1 Thess 4:3–8, which reads as follows:

> For this is God's will: your sanctification—for you to abstain from fornication (*porneia*), for each one of you to know [how] to take his own vessel in holiness and honor, not in passion of lust like also the nations that do not know God, for [each of you] not to transgress and wrong his brother in this matter, because [the] Lord is an avenger in all these things, just as also we forewarned and testified to you. For God did not call us to uncleanness but in holiness. Therefore the one disregarding [this] is not disregarding a human but God, who gives his holy spirit to you.[5]

Because it immediately follows a reference to abstaining from fornication (*porneia*) and is immediately followed by a reference to "passion of lust," most commentators assume that the Greek phrase translated above as "take his own vessel" also has a sexual connotation. Thus, it has been variously interpreted to mean "acquire his own wife," "take control of his own body," or "take control of his own penis." If it means "acquire his own wife," then the reference is clearly to marriage (and presumably sex). In no way, however, does the passage suggest that Paul *hates* sex. Quite to the contrary, if the passage does refer to sex, it associates marriage (and presumably sex) with "sanctification," "holiness," and "honor." To be sure, the translation and interpretation of the key phrase in this passage are uncertain, and it is thus to other pas-

---

*I am assuming that Paul almost certainly was not the author of the Pastoral Letters (1 Timothy, 2 Timothy, and Titus) and that Ephesians, Colossians, and 2 Thessalonians are also most likely non-Pauline. Only Romans, 1 Corinthians, 2 Corinthians, Galatians, Philippians, 1 Thessalonians, and Philemon are authentically Pauline in origin, and it is to these letters alone that we must look for evidence regarding Paul's attitude toward sex.

sages that we must look to find a more certain expression of Paul's attitude toward sex.

1 Corinthians 16:19 and Romans 16:3–4, 7

Paul's letters also contain three more-or-less-incidental references to male-female couples (presumably married and thus presumably involved in a sexual relationship) with whom he has been associated in his work among the churches. These references provide a more certain indication of Paul's attitude toward marriage (and thus, presumably, toward sex) than does 1 Thess 4:3–8. In 1 Cor 16:19 and particularly in Rom 16:3–4, he speaks highly of Prisca and Aquila as his "fellow workers in Christ Jesus" who "risked their necks" for his life and in whose house a church meets. He also refers in Rom 16:7 to another presumably married couple, Andronicus and Junia, as his "kinspeople," his "fellow prisoners," and "noted apostles" who were "in Christ" before he was.* In neither of these references does Paul suggest that marriage (presumably including sexual relations) interferes with the effectiveness or value of the work of these two couples as leaders in the churches or that marriage (presumably including sexual relations) is to be seen in anything less than a positive light.

1 Corinthians 9:5

First Cor 9:5 reads, "Do we not have the right to be accompanied by a sister-wife as also the other apostles and the brothers of the Lord and Cephas?"[6] Here, Paul indicates that "the other apostles," "the brothers of the Lord," and "Cephas" are married and suggests that they are accompanied by their wives as they engage in the work of the churches. In no way does he intimate that marriage (presumably including sexual relations) interferes with the work of ministry in the churches. Indeed, these verses could even be seen as expressing Paul's own wish that he might be accompanied by a wife.

*In the past, many translators and commentators, simply assuming that a woman could not have been an apostle, have argued that the Greek *Jounian* must be the accusative case of an abbreviated form for a *masculine* name. Epp (*Junia*), however, has shown conclusively that *Jounian* is the accusative form of the *feminine* name "Junia."

Romans 1:26–27

Rom 1:26–27 *clearly* does refer to sex or, more specifically, what we would today call homosexual activity. These verses read as follows:

> Because of this, God gave them up to dishonorable passions, for their women exchanged natural relations for unnatural ones, and the men likewise left behind the natural relations with women and were consumed with their passion for one another, men committing shameless acts with men and receiving in themselves the penalty that was necessary for their error.

It is my own judgment that these verses are part of a later non-Pauline interpolation—that is, written by someone other than Paul and secondarily inserted into Paul's letter to the Romans—and thus should not be seen as indicating *Paul's* attitude toward sex.[7] Whether the verses are Pauline or non-Pauline, however, it is important to note that they make an important distinction between sexual relations that are viewed as *natural* (that is, between men and women) and those that are regarded as *unnatural* (that is, between persons of the same sex). It is clear that the author regards *unnatural* sex as improper,[8] but there is nothing in the verses that would indicate a negative attitude toward *natural* sex; indeed, the reference to "impurity" in verse 24, followed by the words about *unnatural* sex, suggests, by way of contrast, that *natural* sex is pure. This is quite in keeping with the possible association of marriage (and presumably sex) with sanctification, holiness, and honor in 1 Thessalonians, with what Paul says about the two couples (presumably married and thus involved in a sexual relationship), Prisca and Aquila and Andronicus and Junia, and with his reference to the married status of other leaders in the churches.

1 Corinthians 7

First Corinthians 7 is the *only* passage containing *possible* evidence that Paul "hated" sex *per se*. It is *only* in this chapter that he expresses a preference for the celibate state, and it is *only* here that he appears to condone marriage simply as a safeguard against sexual immorality (*porneia*). This may suggest that it was *only in Corinth* that Paul encountered a situation calling for such a response. Moreover, it may well be the case that Paul, to some extent, accommodates what he says about sex and marriage in this chapter to what the Corinthians are saying and doing and that this chapter, therefore, represents Paul's response to a specific situation or set of circumstances and does not express his balanced views regarding sex.

In any case, however, the evidence even in 1 Corinthians 7 is by no means as unambiguous as many appear to assume. I note the following points:

1. Scholars are increasingly of the opinion that the words in verse 7:1b, "It is good for a person not to touch a woman,"[9] are not Paul's own words but rather a slogan in vogue among some of the Corinthians that Paul quotes in order to provide a backdrop for his own views, which are somewhat different. Thus, Paul cannot be held responsible for the words in verse 1b.

2. Translated literally, verse 2 reads, "But because of the fornications (Greek: *tas porneias*), let each [man] have his own wife and let each [woman] have her own husband." The definite article and the plural forms (*tas porneias*) suggest that Paul may have in mind certain specific situations in Corinth and that what he says in the chapter is addressed not to believers generally but, at least in large part, to these specific situations and the specific people involved. This possibility is strengthened by the fact that he has already mentioned a case of incest (5:1–5) and, immediately before chapter 7, in 6:12–20, the presence of prostitution (*porneia*) among the Corinthians.

3. In verses 3–5, Paul appears to speak quite positively regarding the role and indeed the necessity of sex within the marriage relationship. Indeed, he *requires* it:

   Let the husband give to the wife what is owed [i.e., her conjugal rights], and likewise also the wife to the husband. The wife does not have authority over her own body, but the husband does; and likewise also the husband does not have authority over his own body, but the wife does. Do not refuse one another except perhaps by agreement for a time in order that you may devote yourselves to prayer, and again come together in order that Satan may not tempt you because of your lack of self-control.

In these verses, it is assumed that both men and women desire to have sexual relations, and nothing is said that would tend to denigrate such desires or such relations. To be sure, Paul sees sexual relations within marriage as a safeguard against *porneia*, but there is also at least the implication that he sees sexual relations within marriage as a way of strengthening and thus preserving the marriage.

4. In 1 Corinthians 7, Paul does not call for the dissolution of marriages, as one might expect if he really *hates* sex. Quite to the contrary, he urges that marriages be preserved if possible—even marriages between believers and non-believers (1 Cor 7:10–24, 39). Regarding such "mixed" marriages he goes so far as to say that the unbelieving spouse is "consecrated" through the believing spouse and that the children of such mixed marriages are "holy" rather than "unclean." These are hardly the words of someone who *hates* sex!

5. In 1 Cor 7:7, Paul appears to regard both the celibate state and the married state as gifts from God ("I wish all people were as I myself am; but each one has his or her own gift, one of one kind and one of another"). Again, this is difficult to reconcile with the view that Paul *hates* sex.

6. Paul's preference for the celibate state appears to be based, at least largely, upon purely pragmatic considerations: the imminent end of the world and a wish for "undivided devotion to the Lord."

Conclusion

In my judgment, an examination of *all* of the relevant evidence by no means indicates that Paul *hated* sex, and this will come as a surprise to many people. On the one hand, he clearly hated *porneia*, and, *in one passage* (1 Corinthians 7), he expressed a preference for the celibate state, spoke of marriage as a safeguard against *porneia*, and suggested that there were pragmatic reasons for remaining unmarried. On the other hand, he did not call for the dissolution of marriages; he spoke of the importance and even necessity of sexual relations between married spouses; he appears to have associated marriage (and thus, presumably, sex) with such terms as "purity," "holiness," and "honor"; he speaks highly of couples (presumably married and thus engaged in sexual relations) who were active leaders in the churches; and, noting that other leaders in the churches are married, he at least hints that he himself might like to be accompanied by a wife as he carries out his responsibilities as an apostle. In short, the evidence regarding Paul's attitude toward sex is mixed.

Paul on Homosexuality[1]

Mainline Christian denominations in this country are bitterly divided over the question of homosexuality. For this reason, it is important to ask what light, if any, the New Testament sheds on this controversial issue. Because, as will be noted below, all of the New Testament passages that possibly relate to homosexuality are in letters attributed to Paul, the question really becomes, what does Paul say—or what do the letters attributed to Paul say—about homosexuality? In this chapter, however, I shall refer to the New Testament rather than to Paul, the letters of Paul, or letters attributed to Paul because to do otherwise might leave the impression that there are references to homosexuality in other parts of the New Testament.

Most people apparently assume that the New Testament expresses strong opposition to homosexuality. The surprise, however, is that this simply is not the case. The six propositions that follow, considered cumulatively, lead to the conclusion that the New Testament does not provide any *direct* guidance for understanding and making judgments about homosexuality in the modern world.

Proposition One
- Strictly speaking, the New Testament says nothing at all about homosexuality.

There is not a single Greek word or phrase in the entire New Testament that should be translated into English as "homosexual" or "homosexuality." In fact, the very notion of homosexuality—like that of heterosexuality, bisexuality, and even sexual orientation—is essentially a modern concept that would simply have been unintelligible to the New Testament writers. The word "homosexuality" came into use only in the latter part of the nineteenth century, and, as Victor Paul Furnish notes, it and related terms "presume an understanding of human sexuality that was possible only with the advent of modern psychological and sociological analysis." In other words, "The ancient writers . . . were operating without the vaguest conception of what we have learned to call 'sexual orientation.'"[2] (Nevertheless, I shall use the terms "homosexual" and "homosexuality" strictly for the sake of convenience.)

Proposition Two

- At most, there are only three passages in the entire New Testament that refer to what we today would call homosexual activity, and, as already noted, all three are in letters attributed to Paul.

None of the four gospels mentions the subject. This means that, so far as we know, Jesus never spoke about homosexuality, and we simply have no way of determining what his attitude toward it might have been. Moreover, there is nothing about homosexuality in the book of Acts, in Hebrews, in Revelation, or in the letters attributed to James, Peter, John, and Jude. Further, homosexuality is not mentioned in ten of the thirteen letters attributed to Paul. It is only in Rom 1:26–27, 1 Cor 6:9–10, and 1 Tim 1:8–11 that there may be references to homosexuality.[3] The paucity of references to homosexuality in the New Testament suggests that it was not a matter of major concern either for Jesus or for the early Christian movement.

Proposition Three

- Two of the three passages that possibly refer to homosexuality are simply catalogs of more-or-less miscellaneous types of behavior that are regarded as unacceptable, with no particular emphasis placed on any individual item in the list.

First Cor 6:9–10 says that certain types of people "will not inherit the kingdom of God." The list of such people begins with fornicators, idolaters, and adulterers, and it ends with thieves, the greedy, drunkards, revilers, and robbers. Near the middle—between adulterers and thieves—are the two Greek words translated in the New Revised Standard Version as "male prostitutes" (that is, homosexual male prostitutes) and "sodomites." But no special emphasis is placed on these people; they are simply listed along with the others. Similarly, 1 Tim 1:8–11 says that the law was given not for good people but for bad people, and it then provides a list, giving representative examples of who these "bad people" might be. Included in the list—this time near the end but again without any special emphasis—is the Greek word translated in the New Revised Standard Version as "sodomites." In both texts, such people are mentioned simply in passing, in catalogs of more-or-less miscellaneous types of unacceptable behavior, but with no special emphasis or attention called to them.

Such lists of vices are fairly common not only in the New Testament and other early Christian literature but also in Mesopotamian, Egyptian, Greco-Roman, and Jewish writings.[4] They appear to have been somewhat stereotypical in nature, representing a kind of laundry list or grab bag of negative labels that could be trotted out and used for rhetorical purposes with little attention to individual items in the lists. As something of an analogy, I cite a passage from Arlo Guthrie's famous ballad, "Alice's Restaurant." In speaking of his own arrest for littering and his assignment to "Group W" in the jail, Guthrie characterizes this group as follows:

> Group W is where they putcha if you may not be moral enough to join the army after committin' your special crime. There was all kinds of mean, nasty, ugly-lookin' people on the bench there. There was mother rapers . . . father stabbers . . . father rapers . . . Father rapers! sittin' right there on the bench next to me!

In somewhat similar fashion, the catalogues in 1 Cor 6:9–10 and 1 Tim 1:8–11 list "all kinds of mean, nasty, ugly-lookin' people."

It should also be noted that different catalogues tend to be remarkably similar in content. They typically list the same kinds of vices. Furthermore, it appears that authors often took over and adapted such lists from earlier documents. This means that the

New Testament writers may not actually have composed the lists in 1 Cor 6:9–10 and 1 Tim 1:8–11. These may simply be conventional lists, taken and adapted from earlier documents and used here for rhetorical purposes. If so, then inclusion of the words translated as "male prostitutes" and "sodomites" may be little more than coincidental.

In any case, neither of the catalogues—1 Cor 6:9–10 or 1 Tim 1:8–11—singles out homosexual activity for any special attention. They just list, in miscellaneous fashion, various types of behaviors that are regarded as unacceptable.

Proposition Four

- It may well be that the two lists of unacceptable behaviors—1 Cor 6:9–10 and 1 Tim 1:8–11—do not refer to homosexuality at all.

The New Revised Standard Version translates 1 Cor 6:9–10 as follows:

> Do you not know that wrongdoers will not inherit the kingdom of God? Do not be deceived! Fornicators, idolaters, adulterers, male prostitutes, sodomites, thieves, the greedy, drunkards, revilers, robbers—none of these will inherit the kingdom of God.

For our purposes, of course, the two key terms are "male prostitutes" and "sodomites." It may well be the case, however, that these are not the most appropriate translations of the underlying Greek in the text.[5]

The Greek word translated as "male prostitutes" is the adjective *malakoi* (plural of *malakos*). This adjective means "soft," as in a soft bed or a soft pillow. When applied to people, it can mean "lazy," "self-indulgent," "cowardly," "lacking in self-control," and the like. When applied to males, it generally refers to what were commonly regarded as feminine-like weaknesses: such men might be regarded as "soft," "flabby," "weak," "cowardly," "unmanly," or "effeminate." But to call a male "effeminate" might or might not carry implications of homosexuality. Sometimes it did, but certainly not always. When it did, it may have referred to the so-called passive or effeminate partner in the homosexual relationship. But we cannot be at all certain that *malakoi* refers to homosexuality in 1 Cor 6:9. It may refer to softness or even effeminacy in some other sense. In any case, the use of the adjective *malakoi* to describe males should probably be seen more as *gyno*phobic than as *homo*phobic. It reflects a fear of women or at least of woman-like—that is, soft or weak—behavior on the part of men.*

People have assumed that *malakoi* does refer to homosexuality in 1 Cor 6:9 primarily because the next term in the list is *arsenokoitai* (defined below)—the assumption being, of course, that the two words are somehow linked in meaning because they appear side by side in the list. This, however, is by no means necessarily the case. "The greedy" and "drunkards" are also juxtaposed in the list, and it would be difficult to see any link between them.

But even if *malakoi* and *arsenokoitai* are somehow linked in meaning, it is not at all clear just how *arsenokoitai* (plural of *arsenokoitēs*) should be translated. It comes from two Greek words: *arsēn*, which means "male" (as opposed to "female"), and *koitē*, which literally means "bed" but by extension can be a euphemism for sexual intercourse (like "going to bed" with someone). This would appear to suggest that *arsenokoitai* refers to males who "go to bed" with other males. But Dale B. Martin has pointed out that the meaning of a compound word cannot necessarily be determined by breaking it apart, looking at the meaning of each of its parts, and then simply combining these meanings to determine the meaning of the compound word. As an example, Martin cites the English word, "understand," which has nothing to do with either "standing" or "being under."[6]

Numerous other examples could be cited, but I want to mention one that is closer to the topic under consideration. The word I have in mind is the vulgar term, "motherfucker." We know what this word means literally. But when people use it, they typically

---

*In terms of the dominant gender stereotyping, feminine-like behavior on the part of men would be seen as weakness, while masculine-like behavior on the part of women would be viewed as hubris.

are not referring to someone who has sexual intercourse with his mother (or even with someone else's mother). In fact, the word normally does not refer to sexual activity at all. Though generally viewed as highly pejorative, it is sometimes used in a more-or-less neutral sense or even, in some circles, as a term of admiration or perhaps affection. The point is, however, that its original sexual meaning is often not apparent in its actual usage. And the same thing may very well be true of the Greek word *arsenokoitai*. Martin has made a study of how the word is actually used in ancient Greek literature. It is a rare word. First Cor 6:9 is probably the earliest occurrence that we have, and most other occurrences are merely quotations from or allusions to 1 Cor 6:9 and/or 1 Tim 1:10 (the only places the word occurs in the New Testament). According to Martin, though, when the word does appear independently, it is typically found in conjunction not with sins of sexual immorality but rather with sins related to *economic* injustice or exploitation. Thus, Martin concludes that *arsenokoitai* most likely refers not to homosexuality as such but rather to the "exploiting of others by means of sex, perhaps but not necessarily by homosexual sex."[7] I would suggest, however, that it might even refer to exploitation that has nothing at all to do with sex. We often use sexual language to talk about things that have nothing to do with sex. For example, someone might say, "I really fucked up!" without having sex in mind at all. Or think about how we sometimes use the word "screw." If I say, "I really got screwed on that business deal," I'm not talking about sex, but I am talking about exploitation. And this is consistent with Martin's conclusion that *arsenokoitai* appears to refer more precisely to exploitation than to sexual activity. The bottom line, however, is that we simply do not know what the word meant or how it was used in the first century.[8]

So, *malakoi* means simply "soft," perhaps "effeminate," and it might or might not refer to homosexuality. And *arsenokoitai*, although it literally means "male-bedders" (that is, "male-fuckers"), might or might not refer explicitly to homosexuality. Therefore, we cannot be certain that 1 Cor 6:9–10 refers to homosexuality at all. The same is true of 1 Tim 1:8–11, which has the word *arseno-*

koitai but not the word *malakoi*. It might not refer to homosexuality either.

Proposition Five

- Even if 1 Cor 6:9–10 and 1 Tim 1:8–11 do refer to homosexuality, what they likely have in mind is not homosexuality per se but rather one particular form of homosexuality that was regarded as especially exploitive and degrading.[9]

Some scholars have suggested that *malakoi* designates attractive young men, or boys, whose sexual services were either purchased or coerced by older men, and that *arsenokoitai* designates these older men who thus "used" or exploited the younger men. According to this interpretation, *malakoi* and *arsenokoitai* do refer to male homosexuality, but the objection is not necessarily to male homosexual activity *per se*, but rather to the prostitution, coercion, and/or exploitation that typically accompanied one particular type of male homosexuality. And this, too, is consistent with Martin's conclusion that *arsenokoitai* refers more specifically to exploitation than it does to sex.* Furthermore, if this is the case, then we simply have no way of knowing what the New Testament writers might have said about a non-exploitive, non-coercive, loving, committed, monogamous homosexual relationship. We cannot know because New Testament writers are not talking about that kind of homosexual relationship.

In the final analysis, then, we cannot be certain that 1 Cor 6:9–10 and 1 Tim 1:8–11 refer to homosexuality at all. And if they

---

*In the ancient world, sex is associated with power. The one who penetrates another person is the one holding power, and the person being penetrated is the powerless one. Thus, just as *malakoi* may be essentially gynophobic, *arsenokoitai* may also be gynophobic and even misogynistic. An *arsenokoitēs* (a "male bedder") may be a male who treats another male as though he were a woman—that is, exercises power over him by penetrating him or in some other way(s) dominating or emasculating him (the implication being, of course, that it is perfectly acceptable and even appropriate to treat females in this way). By the same token, a *malakos* may be a male who either allows himself or is forced/coerced to behave as though he were a female—that is, allows himself or is forced/coerced to be penetrated or in some other way(s) dominated by the *arsenokoitēs*. It was all about *power*, not sex.

do, they do so only in passing in catalogues of more-or-less miscellaneous types of behaviors that are regarded as unacceptable.

Proposition Six

- The one passage in the New Testament that almost certainly does refer to homosexuality is based on some highly debatable presuppositions about its nature and causes.

The passage in question is Rom 1:26–27. Earlier in this chapter, the author is talking about idolatry, the worship of false gods. Then, beginning in verse 24, he talks about the results of idolatry. Verses 24 and 25 identify the results of idolatry as lust, impurity, and the degrading of one's body. Then, verses 26 and 27 spell out in more detail the nature of this lust, impurity, and bodily degradation as follows (New Revised Standard Version):

> For this reason God gave them up to degrading passions. Their women exchanged natural intercourse for unnatural, and in the same way also the men, giving up natural intercourse with women, were consumed with passion for one another. Men committed shameless acts with men and received in their own persons the due penalty for their error.

Following verses 26 and 27, the remainder of the chapter lists some of the other results of idolatry, and the list is rather similar to the catalogues in 1 Cor 6:9–10 and 1 Tim 1:8–11. In other words, homosexuality is but one among other types of unacceptable behaviors.

What must be emphasized, then, is that Rom 1:18–32, taken as a whole, is not about homosexuality. It is about idolatry. The only reason it mentions homosexuality at all is because the author assumes that it is a result of willful idolatry. Knowing full well that there is one true God, people nevertheless freely choose to worship false gods. As punishment for this idolatry, God "gives them up" to homosexual activity. Thus, in a sense, homosexuality is not so much a sin as it is a *punishment* for sin. This should mean, however, that no monotheist would ever take part in homosexual activity—no practicing Jew or Christian or Muslim. Only worshippers of false gods would engage in such activity. This was a fairly common assumption within first-century Judaism, and it is one of the dubious presuppositions that underlie Rom 1:26–27.

Clearly, however, it is not consistent with what we can observe in the world around us.

The passage also makes at least two other assumptions that point to its essential irrelevance so far as modern discussions of homosexuality are concerned. First, it assumes that homosexuality is somehow "unnatural"—contrary to nature—or a better translation would be "beyond what is natural." In other words, it isn't just *unusual* for people to engage in homosexual activity. It is *abnormal*; it *goes beyond* that which is natural. According to the American Psychological Association, however, "most scientists today agree that sexual orientation is most likely the result of a complex interaction of environmental, cognitive, and biological factors."[10] Moreover, psychologists tend to be extremely cautious about using such categories as *natural* and *unnatural*, *normal* and *abnormal* when talking about human behavior.

Second, the passage assumes that homosexuality is an expression of insatiable lust. People turn to homosexual activity because heterosexual activity simply fails to satisfy them. They want more! As Martin points out, it is somewhat like gluttony: gluttony is too much eating, and homosexuality is too much sex.[11] People engage in homosexual activity because they "can't get enough" of sex otherwise. And this, of course, is related to the notion that homosexuality goes beyond that which is natural. *Homo*sexuality is essentially *excessive* sexuality. Together with the author's emphasis on the verb "exchange," this suggests that, in modern terms, the reference in the passage may be more to *bi*sexuality than to *homo*sexuality. If such is the case, then the passage would appear to have little relevance for people whose *sole* orientation is homosexual.

In light of the assumptions that underlie Rom 1:26–27, perhaps the question to be raised when reading these verses is, exactly *what* is it that is being opposed here, and *why* is it being opposed? Is it simply homosexuality *per se*, or is it the idolatry, the *abnormality*, and the insatiable lust that, in the first-century Jewish mind, were associated with homosexual activity? And a second question is this: What would the author of Rom 1:26–27 say about a loving, committed, monogamous homosexual relationship—one that was *not* rooted in idolatry, one that did *not* represent a rejection of one's own true nature, and one that was *not* characterized by excessive lust? I think the answer has to be that we simply do not know, because, once again, the author is talking about something quite different.[12]

Conclusion

- The New Testament really does not provide any direct guidance for understanding and making judgments about homosexuality in the modern world.

To the extent that it does talk about homosexuality, the New Testament appears to be talking about only certain types of homosexuality, and it speaks on the basis of assumptions about homosexuality that are now regarded as highly dubious. Perhaps, then, we could paraphrase what the New Testament says about homosexuality as follows: *If* homosexuality is exploitive, then it is wrong; *if* homosexuality is rooted in idolatry, then it is wrong; *if* homosexuality represents a denial of one's own true nature, then it is wrong; *if* homosexuality is an expression of insatiable lust, then it is wrong. But we could say exactly the same thing about heterosexuality, couldn't we?

If homosexuality is not necessarily any of these things, however, then it would appear that the New Testament has nothing to say about it in any *direct* sense. Speaking specifically of the Pauline letters but in words that are applicable to the New Testament as a whole, the Pauline scholar Victor P. Furnish puts it as follows:

> [Paul's] letters . . . *cannot yield any specific answers to the questions being faced in the modern church.* Shall practicing homosexuals be admitted to church membership? Shall they be accorded responsibilities within a congregation? Shall they be commissioned to the church's ministry? The Apostle never asks or answers these questions . . . On these points there are no proof texts available one way or the other. It is mistaken to invoke Paul's name in support of any specific position on these matters.[13]

In short, there is nothing in the New Testament that tells us *directly* whether homosexuality *per se* is a good thing or a bad thing or simply a fact of life.

To be sure, when we consider its overall message, I think the New Testament provides *indirect* guidance regarding homosexuality. Indeed, it may well be the case that a twenty-first century "Paul" would revise Gal 3:27–28 to read as follows:

> For as many of you as were baptized into Christ have put on Christ. There is neither Jew nor Greek, there is neither slave nor free, there is not male and female, there is neither homosexual nor heterosexual; for you are all one in Christ Jesus.

9

Interpolations in the Letters of Paul[1]

From time to time, various scholars have argued for the pres-ence of one or more "interpolations"—later, non-Pauline addi-tions—in the letters of Paul. A few have maintained that there are many interpolations, but most have focused their attention on individual passages. These passages include, most notably, 1 Thess 2:14–16; 1 Cor 2:6–16; 10:1–22; 11:3–16; 1 Corinthians 13 (actually, 12:31b–14:1b); 1 Cor 14:34–35; 15:29–34; 2 Cor 3:7–18; 6:14–7:1; Gal 2:7b–8; Rom 1:18–2:29; 13:1–7; 8:29–30; and 16:25–27. For the most part, however, arguments for interpolation have not been widely accepted by New Testament scholars. Although many—perhaps most—would agree in principle that there are interpolations in the letters, and there is in fact rather widespread agreement that 1 Cor 14:34–35 and Rom 16:25–27 are interpola-tions, most scholars remain skeptical regarding other proposed interpolations. They see no way to identify such interpolations with any certainty, and they tend to regard arguments for inter-polation as highly speculative and almost inevitably circular in nature.

I am convinced, however, not only that there are sound *a priori* grounds for assuming the presence of interpolations*— probably many interpolations—in the Pauline letters but also that

---

A priori grounds for interpolations are grounds that are based not on evidence within the letters themselves but rather on such considerations as the nature of ancient composition, copying, and editing.

such interpolations can sometimes be identified with a fair degree of certainty. In what follows, therefore, I shall (a) present evidence for the *a priori* probability of interpolations in the letters, (b) argue that three particular passages are in fact interpolations, and (c) briefly suggest some of the implications of interpolations for our understanding of Paul and of early Christianity more generally.[2]

The *A Priori* Probability of Interpolations in the Pauline Letters

There are two primary reasons for the *a priori* assumption of interpolations in the Pauline letters. The first is that scholars have identified numerous apparent interpolations in other ancient literature—Homeric, Classical, Hellenistic, Jewish, and Christian. For example, interpolations have been detected in the Hellenistic literary genre most closely resembling the Pauline letters—namely, the letters of philosophers and moralists to their disciples. Even closer to home, John 7:53–8:11 (the woman taken in adultery) is almost certainly a later addition to the text of the fourth Gospel, and Mark 16:9–20 (the post-resurrection appearances of Jesus) was likely added to the original text of the second Gospel. Furthermore, most scholars agree that large blocks of material were interpolated into the Gospel of Mark to form the Gospels of Matthew and Luke. Because the practice of interpolation was rather widespread in the milieu where Paul's letters were written and circulated, there is good reason to assume, simply on *a priori* grounds, that they too would have been subject to such textual expansion. Indeed, some years ago, two of my colleagues in the Department of Classical Studies at Trinity University—one of them a specialist in Greek literature and the other in Latin literature—independently informed me that they would be quite surprised if there were no interpolations in the letters of Paul.

The second reason for the *a priori* assumption of interpolations in the Pauline letters involves certain aspects of their literary history. Unfortunately, we know considerably less about this history than we might wish, but the following items bear directly on the question of interpolations in the letters:

1. The early churches did not preserve the "autographs" (originals) of any of the letters. All that we have are

handwritten copies, none of which, except for fragments, dates from earlier than around 200 CE, roughly a century and a half after the letters were written. We have no way of knowing how many copies of the letters stand between the autographs and the oldest surviving manuscripts. Moreover, there are numerous textual variations among the surviving manuscripts: no two of them read exactly the same. Thus, despite the conscientious and skilled efforts of generations of textual critics, we can only make educated guesses regarding the text(s) of the letters prior to around 200 CE. The fact that a particular passage appears in the oldest extant manuscript—or, indeed, in all of the surviving manuscripts—indicates no more than that this passage was a part of the text in the late second century. It tells us nothing about whether it appeared in earlier manuscripts or, if so, how much earlier. More specifically, it tells us nothing about whether it was a part of the autograph. At least in theory, the passage could have been added to the text any time between the composition of the letter (around 50–60 CE) and around 200 CE.

2. The church did not preserve early copies of any of the *individual* letters. All we have are *collections* of letters— collections that were assembled, preserved, and transmitted by the early church under the name of Paul. It remains unclear just how such collections came into being—whether through the gradual and informal sharing of individual letters among the churches, by the conscious and deliberate work of one or more collectors, or by some combination of the two. What is clear, however, is that the individual letters were preserved only as parts of collections.

3. These early collections cannot simply be equated with what Paul himself wrote (or dictated). It would be reasonable to assume that they do not include all of Paul's letters, and this assumption is confirmed by references in 1 Cor 5:9–11 and 2 Cor 2:3–4 to letters written by Paul prior to what we know respectively as 1 Corinthians and 2 Corinthians. The early collections of letters, therefore, represent an *abbreviated* Paul. But they also represent an *expanded* Paul—expanded

in the sense that they include letters not actually written by Paul: Hebrews (which doesn't even claim to be written by Paul), almost certainly the three Pastoral Letters (1 Timothy, 2 Timothy, and Titus), and probably Ephesians, Colossians, and 2 Thessalonians. Finally, the collections represent an *edited* Paul—edited at least to the extent that parts of originally different letters were apparently combined to form what now appear as single letters. For example, most scholars agree that 2 Corinthians 1–9 and 2 Corinthians 10–13 come from two different letters, and, indeed, some maintain that 1 and 2 Corinthians contain material from as many as thirteen different letters. Partition theories have also been proposed for Philippians and Romans. It is generally agreed, at least in principle, that such edited collections of the letters would almost certainly include some editorial additions, including but perhaps not limited to brief connecting links. In other words, the "editing" of the letters might very well include the incorporation of additional material—that is, interpolations.

4. We have no way of ascertaining what materials were available to a collector of the letters, or, indeed, what the physical condition of these materials might have been. Authentically Pauline writings, or fragments of the same, may well have been preserved and transmitted along with other materials that were non-Pauline in origin, and it may have been difficult if not impossible to distinguish between the two. Then, when materials were assembled to form a collection of the letters, the tendency almost certainly would have been to err on the side of *in*clusion rather than *ex*clusion lest something that might be Pauline in origin be omitted. Thus, non-Pauline materials may well have been introduced into the letters quite unintentionally, probably on more than one occasion and by more than one hand.

5. The period during which the Pauline letters were being assembled into collections was a time of intense controversy within the church—much of it directly relating to Paul and his letters. As different factions within the church claimed to be authentically Pauline, the Pauline letters would have been particularly susceptible to alteration, including interpolation.

Indeed, we know that at least two significantly different versions of the letters circulated in the second century: a shorter version (no longer extant) accepted by the "heretic" Marcion and a longer version (the only surviving version) recognized by his opponents. Marcion's enemies accused him of excising materials from the letters, he apparently accused them of adding these materials, and there may well have been an element of truth in both accusations. In any case, we cannot simply assume that Marcion's opponents—and perhaps others—made no additions to the text. Indeed, interpolation would be a quite plausible means of adapting the Pauline letters to the changing needs, concerns, and interests of the church, not to mention making them more useful in the ongoing debates that continued for several centuries.

6. The surviving manuscripts of the Pauline letters contain countless variant readings. Indeed, except in the case of brief fragments, no two of the manuscripts—not even of the oldest manuscripts—are identical in every detail. Most of the variants represent simply inadvertent errors on the part of copyists: obvious misspellings, transpositions, omissions, repetitions, and the like. A few, however, appear to represent intentional changes, intended to correct, clarify, or even amplify the text. Included in this latter category are short additions to the text, which can be identified by their being present in some manuscripts but not in others. For example, the benediction that appears before the doxology* of Rom 16:25–27 in some manuscripts and after the doxology in a few is certainly to be regarded as a later addition to the text (see pp. 95–96). Similarly, the appearance in a few manuscripts of the words "and one Holy Spirit, in whom are all things and for whom we exist" at the end of 1 Cor 8:6 is clearly an addition intended to make the verse express a Trinitarian theology (that is, "one God, the Father . . . one

---

*A doxology is a formulaic ascription of glory to God. The doxology in Rom 16:25–27, for example, concludes with "to the only wise God, through Jesus Christ, to whom be the glory forever."

Lord, Jesus Christ . . . and one Holy Spirit"). The presence of such obvious textual variants, including additions to the text, further reinforces the *a priori* probability of interpolations—probably many interpolations—in the Pauline letters.

7. We have no way of knowing what became of either the autographs of the letters or early copies of individual letters—or, indeed, of all copies of the letters dating from before around 200 CE. They may simply have deteriorated and disintegrated from constant use (or from neglect), or they may have perished during the Roman persecutions of the period. There are, however, other possible scenarios. It is quite possible that collections of the letters rendered copies of individual letters—including the autographs—superfluous and that these copies therefore gradually dropped out of use and disappeared. It is also possible, however, that once edited collections began to appear, earlier versions of the letters—whether of individual letters or of collections of letters—were deliberately suppressed and perhaps destroyed by Christians themselves who regarded these earlier versions as defective. Indeed, in a context of intense controversy regarding Paul and his letters, it would by no means be surprising if there were a concerted effort to standardize the text of the letters. In particular, a longer version of a letter would almost certainly have been preferred over a shorter version because of perceived omissions—or even the possibility of omissions—in the latter. This would account for the fact that, despite the numerous textual variants already mentioned, all of the surviving manuscripts are for the most part so remarkably similar in their overall content and wording. It would also explain why no manuscripts dating from before the latter part of the second century have survived. Finally, it would account for the fact that most of the proposed interpolations appear in all of the surviving manuscripts.[3]

8. The text of the Pauline letters prior to the appearance of the earliest surviving edited collection (around 200 CE) remains, probably forever, shrouded in the mists of obscurity. Suppression and destruction of earlier manuscripts (if it

occurred) would suggest, however, that these manuscripts may have differed in significant ways from the standardized text that survived (surely this was the case with Marcion's version, which has not survived); otherwise, it is difficult to understand why they would have disappeared so completely. We know that the surviving version of the Pauline letters includes passages not found in the Marcionite version; it may well also include passages not found in other earlier versions either of the collected letters or of individual letters. Thus, the surviving version may well contain interpolations that appear in all of the extant manuscripts.

In short, it is my judgment that aspects of the literary history of the Pauline letters just mentioned, coupled with the widespread presence of interpolations in other ancient literature, makes it almost certain, simply on *a priori* grounds, that the Pauline letters now contain interpolations—indeed, many interpolations. The question then becomes, of course, whether such interpolations can be identified with any degree of certitude and, if so, how.

As I have already indicated, arguments for interpolation have, for the most part, not been widely accepted by New Testament scholars. There are, however, two exceptions: Rom 16:25–27 and 1 Cor 14:34–35. In what follows, I shall summarize the evidence that these two passages are interpolations and then present arguments for viewing a third passage—1 Corinthians 13—as also an interpolation.

Romans 16:25–27

Rom 16:25–27, which appears in all major translations of the New Testament but is nevertheless widely regarded as an interpolation, reads as follows in the New Revised Standard Version:

> Now to the God who is able to strengthen you according to my gospel and the proclamation of Jesus Christ, according to the revelation of the mystery that was kept secret for long ages but is now disclosed, and through the prophetic writings is made known to all the Gentiles, according to the command of the eternal God, to bring about the obedience of faith—to the only wise God, through Jesus Christ, to whom be the glory forever! Amen.

The reasons for regarding this doxology as an interpolation are the following:

1. It is missing altogether in some manuscripts and other witnesses* to the text of Romans.
2. Although the doxology does appear in the vast majority of the manuscripts, it is variously located—often at the end of chapter 14, at the end of chapter 15 in the oldest surviving manuscript, at the end of chapter 16 in most of the best manuscripts, at the end of both chapters 14 and chapter 16 in a few manuscripts, and at the end of both chapter 14 and chapter 15 in one manuscript.
3. Two textual variants (that is, different readings in different manuscripts) suggest that the verses may, in their original form, have been regarded by some scribes as an inadequate or inappropriate conclusion to Paul's Roman letter: (a) the addition of the words "and the appearance of our Lord Jesus Christ" after "through the prophetic writings," presumably to further Christianize the doxology, and (b) the omission of "to whom" or the substitution of "to him" before "be the glory forever," apparently to make it clear that the ascription of glory was directed toward "the only wise God," not toward "Jesus Christ."
4. All of the other letters attributed to Paul end with a benediction (blessing), not a doxology (ascription of glory), and, indeed, a number of manuscripts have added a benediction in Romans—most of them placing it before the doxology but a few after it.
5. Unlike doxologies within the body of Paul's letters (Gal 1:5; Phil 4:20; and Rom 11:36b), which appear to grow out of and reflect the immediately preceding material, Rom 16:25–27 is a complete, self-contained unit that bears little if any apparent relation to its immediate context and, in this respect, resembles doxologies in the letters attributed to Paul but written by others in his name[4] and other post-Pauline writings (see, for example, Eph 3:20–21 and Jude 24–25).

*Other witnesses to the text are references in early Christian writings not included in the New Testament.

6. Rom 16:25–27 is much longer and syntactically much more complex than the doxologies in Paul's other letters—here, too, resembling doxologies in the pseudo-Pauline writings.

7. Much of the vocabulary of Rom 16:25–27 appears not to be typically Pauline (e.g., "the proclamation of Jesus Christ," "according to the revelation of the mystery," "long ages," "prophetic writings," "according to the command of the eternal God," and "to the only wise God").

8. The notion of a "mystery" that had been hidden but now has been revealed is not found in the other authentic letters of Paul but is characteristic of pseudo-Pauline and other non-Pauline texts such as Colossians, Ephesians, 2 Timothy, Titus, and First Peter.

Separately, each of the above items can be explained more or less adequately without recourse to an interpolation hypothesis, but their cumulative weight has led most scholars to conclude that Rom 16:25–27 is in fact a later, non-Pauline interpolation.

1 Corinthians 14:34–35

A second passage that is rather widely regarded as an interpolation is 1 Cor 14:34–35, which reads as follows in the New Revised Standard Version:

> Women should be silent in the churches. For they are not permitted to speak, but should be subordinate, as the law also says. If there is anything they desire to know, let them ask their husbands at home. For it is shameful for a woman to speak in church.

The reasons for regarding these verses as an interpolation are the following:

1. Although they appear in all extant manuscripts of 1 Corinthians, they are (a) separated from verse 33 by intervals or paragraph markings in the earliest manuscripts, (b) marked in one of the oldest manuscripts by a symbol interpreted by some scholars as indicating awareness of a textual variant (that is, different readings in different manuscripts), and (c) located by a few manuscripts at the very end of chapter 14 rather than between verses 33 and

36. All of this suggests some uncertainty on the part of early scribes regarding the relationship of the verses to their immediate context in 1 Corinthians 14.

2. The verses represent a complete, self-contained unit of material that could easily stand alone if removed from its present context.

3. The content of the verses has little if anything to do with Paul's discussion of "spiritual gifts" that immediately precedes and follows. Indeed, they interrupt this discussion with their apparently irrelevant prohibition of women speaking in church, and their removal would in no way affect the flow of Paul's discussion.

4. Although 1 Corinthians 12–14 as a whole appears to be addressed specifically to the Corinthian church, verse 34 commands women to be silent "in the churches" (plural), thus suggesting a wider intended audience for verses 34 and 35.

5. The sentiments expressed in the verses appear to be at odds with Paul's views as expressed elsewhere in his letters. Even the immediate context in chapter 14 apparently assumes that women are included among those who speak in church (note the "all" in verses 5, 18, 23, 24, and 31 and the "each one" of verse 26). What is more important is that the verses contradict not only Paul's avowed egalitarianism as articulated in Gal 3:27–28 (in Christ, there is no distinction between Jew and Greek, slave and free, male and female) but also his surprisingly even-handed and egalitarian discussion of sex, marriage, and divorce in 1 Corinthians 7 and the very positive and non-discriminatory manner in which he speaks of various women with whom he has been associated in the work of the church. The verses also contradict 1 Cor 11:4–5, which speaks explicitly of *both men and women* praying and prophesying (presumably in church), but this may be irrelevant because some scholars—myself included—regard 11:4–5 as part of another later, non-Pauline interpolation (11:3–16). In any case, it stretches the imagination to think that the Paul who wrote Gal 3:27–28 and 1 Corinthians 7 and who spoke so positively about the activity of individual

women in the churches might also have written (or approved) the sentiments expressed in 1 Cor 14:34–35! This suggests that the verses were written by someone other than Paul.

6. The verses are reminiscent of 1 Tim 2:11–12: "Let a woman learn in silence, in all submissiveness. And I do not permit a woman to teach or to have authority over a man, but to be in silence." Because 1 Timothy is widely regarded as pseudonymous (that is, written in Paul's name by someone other than Paul), this suggests that the sentiments expressed in 1 Cor 14:34–35 reflect the views of post-Pauline Christians who were troubled by the fact that women were assuming or seeking to assume leadership roles in the church.

7. Although Clement of Alexandria (who died around 215 CE) cites 1 Cor 14:6, 9, 10, 13, 20 and discusses the behavior of women in church, he does not refer to 1 Cor 14:34–35, and the earliest extant citation of these verses is apparently by Tertullian (around 160–240 CE). This suggests that the verses may not originally have been a part of Paul's Corinthian letter.

8. At a number of points, the vocabulary of the verses appears not to be characteristically Pauline: (a) The verb translated as "be silent" occurs only three times elsewhere in the undisputed Pauline letters—at Rom 16:25 (as already indicated, part of an almost certainly non-Pauline interpolation) and 1 Cor 14:28, 30 (shortly before 14:34–35). (b) The verb translated as "permitted" is found elsewhere in the undisputed letters only at 1 Cor 16:7, where it is in the active voice (not the passive as in 14:34) and refers not to a regulation regarding human conduct (as in 14:34) but simply to the Lord "permitting" Paul to visit the Corinthians. (c) The verb translated as "be subordinate" appears a number of times in the Pauline letters, but it almost always refers to subordination to God, to Christ, to God's law, to God's righteousness, or to "futility." Apart from 1 Cor 14:34, it refers to subordination to humans at only three places, the first of which is regarded by some as part of a non-Pauline

interpolation: Rom 13:1, 5 (governing authorities), 1 Cor 14:32 (prophets), and 1 Cor 16:16 (Christian leaders). (d) The verb translated as "ask" appears elsewhere in the undisputed letters only at Rom 10:20, in a quotation from Isa 65:1. (e) The adjective translated as "shameful" is found elsewhere in the undisputed letters only at 1 Cor 11:16, which is part of another suspected non-Pauline interpolation. (f) The clause translated as "as the law also says" reflects a different attitude toward the law than is found elsewhere in Paul's letters, where Paul typically expresses a rather negative view of the law, or, when he does appeal to scripture to support an argument, cites a particular passage (for example, 1 Cor 9:8–9 and 14:21) rather than simply referring to "the law." All of this suggests that verses 34–35 were composed by someone other than Paul.

As in the case of Rom 16:25–27, it is the cumulative weight of these various items, not individual items considered separately, that has led many scholars to conclude that 1 Cor 14:34–35 is a later, non-Pauline interpolation. The supposition is that some reader of the letter, perhaps in light of 1 Tim 2:11–12, added these words in the margin or between the lines of a manuscript in order to clarify and limit Paul's apparent approval of both men and women prophesying and speaking in tongues in church—the intention being to explain that when Paul said "all" he really meant "all men." Later scribes, perhaps also aware of 1 Tim 2:11–12 and assuming that the words reflected the actual views of Paul, would then have incorporated them into the text of 1 Corinthians— sometimes at the end of chapter 14 but most often after verse 33.

1 Corinthians 13

Although both Rom 16:25–27 and 1 Cor 14:34–35 are widely regarded as interpolations, the same cannot be said regarding any of the other proposed interpolations. One of these is 1 Corinthians 13 (actually, 12:31b–14:1b), the well-known and beloved paean to love. I am convinced that a strong case can be made—and, in fact, has been made—for viewing this chapter as an interpolation. The arguments are the following:

1. The passage is in no way dependent on chapters 12 or 14 for its meaning and can quite easily stand alone—indeed, it often does stand alone—as an independent, self-contained unit. This is attested, for example, by its frequent use in marriage ceremonies.

2. The removal of 12:31b–14:1b leaves a smooth transition from 12:31a to 14:1c, which then reads, "But strive for the greater gifts, and especially that you may prophesy." The repetitive words in 14:1b ("but strive for the spiritual gifts") apparently represent an interpolator's attempt to link chapter 14 to chapter 12 following the interruption of 12:31b–14:1b. Similarly, 12:31b ("And I will show you a still more excellent way") likely represents the interpolator's attempt to link the encomium on love with 12:31a ("but strive for the greater gifts"). Indeed, the reason for placing the interpolation here rather than at the end of chapter 14, where it would fit much better, may well have been the words, "But strive for the greater gifts." Love would then be presented as the "greater gift"—a point that is made explicit in 13:13, where love is portrayed as "greater"[5] than either faith or hope.

3. Both the literary form and the style of the passage differ markedly from those of chapters 12 and 14. Whether it be regarded as a poem, a hymn, a prose-poem, or something else, it clearly represents a literary genre that is far removed from that of chapters 12 and 14, with their detailed and didactic attention to "spiritual gifts." Moreover, the passage, unlike chapters 12 and 14, contains not a single imperative verb, and, again unlike chapters 12 and 14, the verbs tend to be in the first person, not the second or third person.

4. As regards content, the passage interrupts Paul's discussion of spiritual gifts and their place in public worship with what is essentially a critique of spiritual gifts that disregards them as of relatively little importance. Furthermore, the emphasis is now on the individual rather than the community. The passage might be appropriate *following* chapter 14 as a way of saying that discussions of the relative value of spiritual gifts would become unnecessary and even irrelevant if love prevailed. Coming *between* chapters 12 and 14, however, it

turns the latter chapter into an anti-climatic relapse into the controversy that has just been declared irrelevant.

5. A number of words and metaphors in the passage appear to be non-Pauline. Indeed, the twelve Greek words translated as follows in the New Revised Standard Version appear nowhere else in the authentic Pauline letters: "show" (12:31b), "noisy" (13:1), "gong" (13:1), "clanging" (13:1), "cymbal" (13:1), "remove" (13:2), "is kind" (13:4), "is boastful" (13:4), "is irritable" (13:5), "will cease" (13:8), "mirror" (13:12), and "dimly" (13:12). In addition, four words appear only once elsewhere in the authentic letters: "mountains" (13:2), "give away" (13:3), "is patient" (13:4), and "is rude" (13:5). Further, certain metaphors are not found elsewhere in the authentic letters: "show . . . a way" (12:31b), "a noisy gong or a clashing cymbal" (13:1), "faith so as to remove mountains" (13:2), "see in a mirror" (13:12), and "face to face" (13:12). So much apparently non-Pauline vocabulary suggests non-Pauline authorship of the passage.

6. Not only does the content of the passage interrupt the context in which it appears but certain substantive features of the content are surprising and appear non-Pauline: (a) the complete absence of Christology or, indeed, of any reference at all to Christ (or God!), (b) the subordination of faith to love, (c) the apparent definition of faith as that which enables one "to remove mountains," (d) the somewhat gnostic* nature of the eschatology, in which the ideal state is that of perfect knowledge, and (e) as already noted, the substantive tension between the passage and Paul's discussion of spiritual gifts that immediately precedes and follows.

On the basis of the cumulative weight of these considerations, I conclude that 1 Cor 12:31b–14:1b is likely a later, non-Pauline interpolation.

---

*"Gnostic" derives from the Greek word for "knowledge" and refers to the notion, rather widespread in antiquity, that salvation is based not on works or faith but rather on supernaturally-revealed knowledge of one's own true nature and the true nature of reality.

Implications of Interpolations for Understanding Paul and Early Christianity

The apparent presence of interpolations in the Pauline letters has at least the following implications for our understanding of Paul and of early Christianity more generally:

1. Obviously, it sheds light on the views of Paul himself. For example, if both 1 Cor 14:34–35 and 1 Cor 11:3–16 are later, non-Pauline interpolations, as I believe them to be, then there is not a single passage in the authentic letters that advocates male dominance and female subordination. Quite to the contrary, Paul appears remarkably egalitarian in his understanding of the status and role of women. Similarly, if Rom 13:1–7 is a later non-Pauline interpolation, as I believe it to be, then Paul nowhere advocates unquestioning subjection to the civil authorities. Further, if 1 Thess 2:14–16 is an interpolation, as I believe it to be, then it becomes much more difficult to accuse Paul of anti-Semitism, particularly in light of his agonizing struggle in Romans 9–11 to relate his faith in Christ to his Jewish heritage. Another example: if 1 Cor 15:29–34 is an interpolation, as I believe it to be, then Paul is not the author of the problematic text about "being baptized on behalf of the dead." A final example: if Rom 8:28–30 is an interpolation, as I believe it to be, then Paul is not the precursor of the type of Calvinist scholastic predestinarianism that has characterized some branches of Protestantism. Such examples, of course, point to the danger of identifying particular passages as interpolations simply as a way of "getting Paul off the hook." Indeed, a friend of mine (himself a noted New Testament scholar) once said to me, "Every time you find a passage you don't like, you decide that Paul didn't write it." This danger can be offset, however, by a rigorous application of the kinds of criteria exemplified above in my discussion of Rom 16:25–27, 1 Cor 14:34–35, and 1 Corinthians 13 and by a determined willingness to follow the evidence wherever it may lead. This means that we may end up identifying passages as interpolations that

we wish Paul *had* written—passages such as 1 Corinthians 13.

2. The apparent presence of interpolations in the Pauline letters also sheds light on some of the interests, concerns, problems, and needs of the post-Pauline churches. These would include the appropriate status and role of women (1 Cor 14:34–35 and 1 Cor 11:3–16), relations between Christians and civil authorities (Rom 13:1–7), relations between Christians and Jews (1 Thess 2:14–16), and the fate of the unbaptized dead (1 Cor 15:29–34). To the extent that interpolations represent *deliberate* insertions of non-Pauline material into the Pauline letters, their presence would also indicate one of the ways in which post-Pauline Christians attempted to deal with such interests, concerns, problems, and needs—namely, by adding to the letters materials in which "Paul" addresses the matters at hand. Another way, of course, was by writing new letters—*pseudonymous* letters—in Paul's name.

3. The apparent presence of interpolations in the Pauline letters also sheds light on the surprising freedom with which early Christians handled their texts. Far from regarding these texts as sacrosanct, written in stone, they altered them in various ways to meet the changing interests, concerns, problems, and needs of the churches, and these alterations included the incorporation of new material into the texts.

In short, if—as is almost certainly the case—there are indeed interpolations in the Pauline letters, it is important to identify as many of them as possible in order to expand our understanding of Paul himself and of early Christianity more generally.

Paul and Other New Testament Authors

It is no exaggeration to say that Paul dominates the New Testament. Thirteen of its twenty-seven books claim him as their author,[1] roughly two-thirds of another (Acts of the Apostles) has him as its main character, still another (2 Peter) briefly mentions him by name, and a compelling argument can be made that two others (James and Matthew) have Paul, his letters, and/or Pauline Christianity in mind in some of what they say.[2] An examination of these other writings, however, leads to some surprising results so far as portrayals of and attitudes toward Paul are concerned.

Acts of the Apostles

In Acts of the Apostles, the first reference to Paul (who, however, is referred to as "Saul"),* comes at Acts 7:58, which says that those

---

*Despite the popular notion that the name of the character in question was "Saul" before his "conversion" and was changed to "Paul" at the time of the "conversion," this has no basis either in Acts or in Paul's letters. Until Acts 13:9 (four chapters after the account of his "conversion"), he is always referred to as "Saul." There, the words, "And Saul, the one also [called] Paul," mark a turning point, after which the name is always "Paul." No explanation is given for the change. In the letters, the name is always "Paul." A very few scholars have suggested that "Saul" and "Paul" were actually two different people, whose stories have somehow been conflated in Acts; this, however, is highly unlikely.

who stoned Stephen laid their coats at his feet. Then, Acts 8:1 reports that Saul approved the murder of Stephen. The next reference to Saul is Acts 9:1–30, which recounts his trip to Damascus to arrest Christ-believers and his "conversion" on the way,* his preaching in and escape from Damascus, his arrival and activity in Jerusalem, and his departure for Tarsus. Saul is not mentioned from 9:31 through 11:24 but reappears at 11:25–30, where Barnabas seeks him out in Tarsus, brings him to Antioch, and the two of them then carry famine relief to the believers in Judea. He is not mentioned in chapter 12 but reappears at 13:1. From this point until the end of Acts (13:1–28:31), all of the narrative focuses on the activity of Saul/Paul.

Surprisingly, however, a close reading of this narrative reveals a rather different portrait of Paul than that which appears in his own letters.[3] The differences include the following:

1. In his letters, Paul insists, sometimes vehemently, that he, like other leaders such as Cephas, James, and John, is an *apostle*—that is, a duly authorized Christian *envoy*.[4] Acts, however, does not portray him as an apostle, reserving this title almost exclusively for the original leaders of the church in Jerusalem.[5]
2. In Galatians, Paul insists that he received the gospel not from humans but rather by divine revelation.[6] Acts, however, suggests that he was dependent on other Christian leaders for his knowledge of the gospel.[7]
3. In Galatians, Paul insists that, immediately following his "conversion," he "did not confer with any human being" but rather went to Arabia, then returned to Damascus, and—not until three years later—went to Jerusalem (presumably for the first time), where he stayed for fifteen days but saw none of the apostles except Cephas and James and was "unknown

*The term "conversion" is commonly applied to the experience that made Paul a Christ-believer. The term is misleading, however, because Paul did not move from irreligion to religion, nor did he, at least in his own mind, move from one religion (Judaism) to another religion (Christianity). In what follows, however, I shall use the term "conversion" (in quotation marks) simply for convenience.

by sight to the churches of Judea."[8] In Acts, however, Paul was baptized by Ananias in Damascus, spent "some days" with "the disciples" in Damascus, and then went to Jerusalem, where he spent time with the believers there (Acts 9:10–30).[9]

4. In his letters, Paul strongly implies that he visited Jerusalem a total of only three times.[10] Acts, however, not only indicates that he resided in Jerusalem prior to his "conversion"[11] but also reports that he returned to Jerusalem five times afterward[12] and that he had a nephew in the city,[13] thereby suggesting that his ties with Jerusalem (and presumably with the leaders of the church in Jerusalem) were much stronger than he himself reports in his letters.

5. In his letters, Paul apparently struggles to maintain a balance between proper respect for the leaders of the church in Jerusalem and his own independence as an apostle.[14] Acts, however, portrays Paul as, in fact, subject to the jurisdiction of—or at least willing to follow the advice of—the Jerusalem church leadership.[15]

6. In his letters (particularly Galatians and Romans), Paul places great emphasis on "justification by faith."[16] In Acts, however, the idea appears only twice, in an attenuated form, once on the lips of Paul[17] and once on the lips of Peter.[18]

7. In his letters, Paul indicates that he and his views were the subject of intense controversy throughout his career.[19] Acts, however, plays down this controversy, devoting only one chapter (chapter 15) to an episode that ended in an amicable compromise between Paul and the leaders of the church in Jerusalem and then briefly alluding to controversy in 21:18–26.

8. In Galatians, Paul reports a division of labor whereby he and Barnabas would carry the gospel to the Gentiles while James, Cephas (Peter), and John would go to the Jews.[20] In Acts, however, Peter is portrayed as the one chosen by God to carry the gospel to the Gentiles.[21]

9. Because of his letters, we know Paul not only as a great missionary but also as a rather frequent writer (or dictator) of letters. Acts, however, does not so much as mention that Paul ever wrote letters.*

In short, the book of Acts (a) denies Paul the title of *apostle*,† (b) reports Paul's activity following his "conversion" in a way that contradicts Paul's own narrative, (c) suggests that Paul was dependent on other people for his knowledge of the gospel and that he continued to be subordinate to the Jerusalem church leadership throughout his life, (d) portrays Peter, not Paul, as the chosen pioneer in the mission to the Gentiles, (e) downplays both Paul's major theme of justification by faith and the controversial nature of his message, and (f) makes no mention whatsoever of his letters.‡ In my judgment, all of this should be seen as an attempt to domesticate Paul—that is, to draw him into the mainstream of the emerging proto-catholic Christian consensus. In order to do this, however, the author must portray Paul in a quite different light than he presents himself in his letters.§

2 Peter

Second Peter is widely regarded as pseudonymous, and it may be the latest of the New Testament writings.[22] Other than the thirteen

---

*There is a growing consensus among New Testament scholars that the author of Acts was familiar with a collection of Paul's letters. If so, this author may have deliberately omitted any mention of the letters precisely because they present such a different portrait of Paul.

†It is noteworthy that Marcion, an early-to-mid-first-century "heretic," regarded Paul as the *only* true apostle and thought that the other so-called apostles had misunderstood Jesus and his message. For the argument that Acts was written, at least in part, to counter the teachings of Marcion, see Tyson, *Marcion and Luke-Acts*.

‡Marcion, by way of contrast, regarded *only* the letters of Paul and a shorter version of the Gospel of Luke as scripture (it is a matter of scholarly debate whether Marcion truncated a longer version of Luke, his opponents expanded a shorter version of Luke, or both).

§More and more scholars are now dating Acts in the early second century. My own view is that it might be as late as mid-second century, in which case its anti-Marcionite and proto-catholic agenda becomes even more likely.

letters attributed to Paul and the book of Acts, it is the only writing in the New Testament that mentions Paul by name. This occurs in 2 Pet 3:15b–17, which reads as follows in the New Revised Standard Version:

> So also our beloved brother Paul wrote to you according to the wisdom given to him, speaking of this as he does in all his letters. There are some things in them hard to understand, which the ignorant and unstable twist to their own destruction, as they do the other scriptures. You therefore, beloved, since you are forewarned, beware that you are not carried away with the error of the lawless and lose your own stability.

This passage is by no means an enthusiastic endorsement of Paul or his letters. Moreover, it appears to be irrelevant so far as the remainder of the book is concerned, and it raises a number of questions:

1. Why—if Paul's letters are so difficult to understand and subject to dangerous misunderstanding, and, given the fact that the reference to Paul and the letters appears to be irrelevant so far as the remainder of the book is concerned—is this reference included in 2 Peter at all? The most plausible answer is that the letters are being used by the "false teachers" against whom the author of 2 Peter writes and this author wants to enlist Paul and his letters in the battle against them. This is made difficult, however, by the fact that "there are some things in [the letters] hard to understand, which the ignorant and unstable twist to their own destruction." Thus, the author cites Paul and his letters but also warns against their "misuse." This suggests that the author of 2 Peter considers Paul and his letters a force to be reckoned with, not to be ignored, but also dangerous.
2. What is the "this" (Greek: "these things") about which Paul is said to speak in all his letters? Earlier in chapter 3, the subject is the coming of "the day of the Lord" (verses 1–13), but this is hardly something that Paul addresses in *all* of his letters. More broadly, 2 Peter is directed against "false teachers" and "false teachings," and this subject is addressed in some of Paul's letters.[23]

3. Does the phrase translated as "the other scriptures" (the Greek reads literally "the other writings" [tas loipas graphas]) mean that Paul's letters are now regarded as what we would call "scripture"? At some point, the Greek *graphē* came to mean "scripture" (just as the Latin *scriptura* at some point came to mean "scripture"). Whether this was true when 2 Peter was written is uncertain.[24]
4. What are the "some things" in Paul's letters that are "hard to understand"? Does the reference to "the lawless" in verse 17 point to the Pauline notion of freedom from the law as the point at issue?
5. Who are "the ignorant and unstable" who "twist [these things] to their own destruction"? Again, does the reference to "the lawless" in verse 17 point to people who accept Paul's views regarding freedom from the law?
6. In short, is the reference to "the lawless" a veiled allusion to Paul's argument that Christians are free from the law?

Regardless of how these questions are answered, 2 Pet 3:15b–17 (a) indicates that Paul's letters have become both in some sense authoritative for various Christian groups and a topic of debate among these groups, (b) suggests that the debate may have something to do with "law," and (c) notes the seriousness of the debate by the use of such epithets as "the ignorant and unstable" and "the lawless" and by predicting the "destruction" of such people. In short, it appears that, although the author of 2 Peter refers to Paul as "our beloved brother"[25] and may even regard Paul's letters as in some sense scripture, this author is nevertheless uneasy regarding some of the content of the letters—including perhaps Paul's teaching regarding freedom from the law— which lends itself to misuse by "the ignorant and unstable." Perhaps an appropriate summary of this author's attitude toward Paul and his letters would be the following: "Paul is 'our beloved brother,' and his letters are important, but they must be handled with care because they can easily be misunderstood."

James

Scholars are divided regarding the authorship and date of James. Some attribute it to James the brother of Jesus and date it to roughly the same time as Paul's letters. Most, however, view it as pseudonymous and date it in the late first or early second century.[26] In Jas 2:14–26, the author argues against what might be perceived as Paul's teaching regarding faith and works. The passage reads as follows in the New Revised Standard Version:

> What good is it, my brothers and sisters, if you say you have faith but do not have works? Can faith save you? If a brother or sister is naked and lacks daily food, and one of you says to them, "Go in peace; keep warm and eat your fill," and yet you do not supply their bodily needs, what is the good of that? So faith by itself, if it has no works, is dead. But someone will say, "You have faith and I have works." Show me your faith apart from your works, and I by my works will show you my faith. You believe that God is one; you do well. Even the demons believe—and shudder. Do you want to be shown, you senseless person, that faith apart from works is barren? Was not our ancestor Abraham justified by works when he offered his son Isaac on the altar? You see that faith was active along with his works, and faith was brought to completion by the works. Thus the scripture was fulfilled that says, "Abraham believed God, and it was reckoned to him as righteousness," and he was called the friend of God. You see that a person is justified by works and not by faith alone. Likewise, was not Rahab the prostitute also justified by works when she welcomed the messengers and sent them out by another road? For just as the body without the spirit is dead, so faith without works is also dead.

It is clear that the author of this passage is arguing against *someone* who says that a person is justified by *faith* and *not* by works. In my judgment, this *someone* would almost certainly be either Paul or Pauline Christians (that is, Christians claiming to follow Paul's teachings). In Rom 4:3, Paul quotes Gen 15:6 ("Abraham believed God, and it was reckoned to him as righteousness") to support his argument that a person is justified *by faith and not by works* (the Greek word *dikaiosynē* can be translated as either "righteousness" or "justification"). In Jas 2:23, however, the author quotes *precisely the same verse* to support *his* argument "that a person is justified *by works and not by faith alone.*" In order for the argument to work, however, the author has to preface the Genesis citation with the following:

Was not our ancestor Abraham justified by works when he offered his son Isaac on the altar? You see that faith was active along with his works, and faith was brought to completion by the works.[27]

To be sure, Paul and James appear to be working with different definitions of both "faith" and "works,"[*] but it is clear that Jas 2:14–26 does not agree with Paul regarding the place of each in relation to a person's justification/righteousness. This indicates that Paul's views were controversial in the early church—something that is evident already in Paul's own letters and is even mentioned but then glossed over in the book of Acts. Like the authors of Acts and 2 Peter, the author of James is uncomfortable with Paul's version of Christianity.[28] Indeed, the difference between James and Paul's letters is so great that Martin Luther, that great champion of "justification by faith alone," is famously reported to have referred to James as "an epistle of straw."

Matthew

The Gospel of Matthew (which almost certainly was not written by the Apostle Matthew)[†] contains a passage that appears to be a direct attack on Paul's position regarding the Law. The passage is Matt 5:17–20, which reads as follows in the New Revised Standard Version:

> Do not think that I have come to abolish the law or the prophets; I have come not to abolish but to fulfill. For truly I tell you, until heaven and earth pass away, not one letter, not one stroke of a letter, will pass from the law until all is accomplished. Therefore, whoever breaks one of the least of these commandments, and teaches others to do the same, will be called least in the kingdom of heaven; but whoever does them and teaches them will be called great in the kingdom of heaven. For I tell you, unless your

*For James, "faith" means intellectual assent to propositions such as the belief "that God is one"; for Paul, "faith" means trusting/faithful obedience. For James, "works" means deeds of love and mercy and obedience to God; for Paul, "works" means obedience to Torah.

†The titles, "According to Matthew," "According to Mark," "According to Luke," and "According to John" were all added long after the gospels were written.

righteousness exceeds that of the scribes and Pharisees, you will never enter the kingdom of heaven.

In Gal 3:19–26, Paul says that the law "was added because of transgressions, *until* the offspring would come to whom the promise had been made"—that is, Christ; that "we were imprisoned and guarded under the law *until* faith should be revealed"; that "the law was our disciplinarian *until* Christ came"; and "*now* that faith has come, we are *no longer* subject to a disciplinarian" (emphasis added). More succinctly, in Rom 10:4, he declares that "Christ is the end of the law."[29]

In Matt 5:17–18, however, Jesus declares, "I have come not to abolish [the law or the prophets] but to fulfill [them]," and "not one letter, not one stroke of a letter, will pass from the law until all is accomplished." He also warns that "whoever breaks one of the least of these commandments, and teaches others to do the same, will be called least in the kingdom of heaven." This author also insists that the "righteousness" of Christians must *exceed* that of the scribes and Pharisees ("righteousness" is the translation of the same Greek word, *dikaiosynē*, that is translated as "justification" in Paul's letters), and, it must be remembered, the scribes and Pharisees were the people who were most diligent in following the mandates of the law. Clearly, the author of Matthew is arguing against *someone* who says or implies that the law has been abolished. In my judgment, this *someone* can only be Paul and/or Pauline Christians.

Summary and Conclusion

The book of Acts denies Paul the title of *apostle*, suggests that he was dependent on other Christian leaders for his knowledge of the gospel and continued to be subordinate to them throughout his life, makes Peter (not Paul) the first missionary to the Gentiles, glosses over the controversial nature of Paul's message and activity, and makes no mention whatsoever of Paul's letters. Second Peter says that some of the things in Paul's letters are subject to misunderstanding by "the ignorant and unstable," suggests that "lawlessness" (Paul's doctrine of freedom from the Law?) may be at the heart of the misunderstanding, and threatens destruction for those who are misled. The book of James insists, contrary to Paul's teaching, that *both* faith *and* works are necessary for justification, citing the same verse in Genesis that Paul uses as a proof text. The Gospel of Matthew insists that the Law is still in effect and that whoever breaks it any point or teaches others to break it (Paul and/or his followers?) will be least in the Kingdom of Heaven.

I find it interesting that neither Acts, James, nor Matthew makes any reference to Paul's letters. If the authors were familiar with or aware of the letters, this may suggest that they considered them dangerous and preferred that people not read them. Further, I find it interesting that neither James nor Matthew even mentions Paul by name. This may suggest that the authors of these writings preferred that neither Paul's letters nor Paul himself be brought to the attention of the readers. In any case, I think it is clear that, in somewhat different ways, the authors of Acts, 2 Peter, James, and Matthew were all uncomfortable with Pauline Christianity. And this may come as a surprise to many readers!

Epilogue

I have lived with Paul and his letters for a *very* long time! I was born more than eight decades ago and grew up in a devoutly conservative—I would even say fundamentalist—Presbyterian family. I regularly attended Sunday School and church and participated in Summer Vacation Bible School during my younger years and Youth Fellowship in my high school years. I learned a lot about Paul as I was growing up, although most of it—for example, his "Damascus Road Conversion Experience" and his "Three Missionary Journeys"—came not from his own letters but rather from the book of Acts, which I have now come to regard as an untrustworthy source of information regarding Paul. Thus, in the years that have followed, I have been compelled to *unlearn* a lot of what I had *learned* about Paul and his letters.

The unlearning process began at Austin College (a Presbyterian-related institution), where, as an undergraduate student, I majored in religion and took a course on "Pauline Literature." There, for the first time, I began to realize that Paul may not have written all of the letters that bear his name—that some of them may be pseudonymous. Then, as a student at Austin Presbyterian Theological Seminary, I took courses on "The Theology of Paul," "Ephesians," and "Colossians" and wrote my senior thesis on "The Pauline Doctrine of Reconciliation." I had no courses on Paul in my PhD program at Duke University, but I took a course on "Biblical Theology," and it was there that I was introduced to Rudolf Bultmann and his call for "demythologizing" the New Testament.

During my forty-year career as a member of the Trinity University faculty, I taught a course on "Paul and His Letters" almost every year. I have published numerous scholarly articles on Paul and the letters, as well as two books: *Interpolations in the*

Pauline Letters (2001)[1] and *Paul and His Legacy: Collected Essays* (2015).[2]

Over the years, I have gradually come to accept and recognize the implications of the preliminary observations regarding Paul's letters that are set forth in the Introduction to this book: (1) Paul's letters were not written for us and must, in various ways, be translated and demythologized if they are to be meaningfully understood, (2) they are genuine letters, not comprehensive and systematic statements of Paul's theology, (3) they are occasional letters, intended to address specific issues and problems, and were not intended to be scripture, (4) some of Paul's letters have not survived, (5) some of the letters attributed to Paul are probably pseudonymous (written by others using Paul's name), and (6) we have the letters only as they were preserved, copied by hand, transmitted, assembled into a collection, and edited by early Christians. This last observation has been particularly important for me, as much of my scholarship over the past forty years has been devoted to identifying interpolations (later additions) in the Pauline letters, of which I am convinced that there are many.

As I have continued to study Paul's letters, I have become convinced that some of the charges often made against him simply are not true: Paul was *not* anti-Semitic, misogynistic, or homophobic; he did *not* hate sex; he did *not* call for unquestioning obedience to civil authorities; he did *not* unambiguously accept the institution of slavery; and he was not a "hell fire and damnation" preacher.[3] I have also come to recognize that Paul's apparent lack of interest both in biographical details regarding the historical Jesus and in notions of repentance and forgiveness likely stems from his basic conviction that people are *justified* (that is, brought into right relationship with God) not by anything they themselves do but solely through *pistis Christou* (translated either as "faith in Christ" or, more accurately in my judgment, as "Christ's [own] faith/faithfulness"). Moreover, it has become apparent to me that Paul's thinking about certain topics developed or changed from his earlier to his later letters. For example, it appears that, perhaps as a result of his near-death experience in Ephesus, his vision of "the end time"—his eschatology—shifted from what scholars call an "imminent" eschatology to a more "futuristic" eschatology. Moreover, probably because of his basic conviction regarding justification through *pistis Christou*, Paul appears, in his later letters, to have been moving in the direction of universalism (the belief that *everyone* ultimately will be saved).

The more I have studied the letters of Paul, the more I have come to recognize and appreciate not only the profundity and complexity of his thinking but also his flexibility and his openness. I have also become increasingly aware of the depth of his passion—whether expressed as love and gratitude or as hurt and anger. More and more, I see Paul as a very real human being with very real virtues and flaws. In the final analysis, though, I think F. F. Bruce captured the essence of Paul's thought, character, and humanity with the title of his book, *Paul, Apostle of the Heart Set Free*.[4] I continue to learn from Paul's letters!

Notes

Preface

1. In addition, although it does not mention Paul by name, 1 Peter appears to have been heavily influenced by Paul and/or his letters and is sometimes referred to—along with 1 and 2 Timothy, Titus, Ephesians, Colossians, and 2 Thessalonians—as one of the *Paulinist* writings. Moreover Pauline influence can almost certainly be seen in the Gospel of Luke and perhaps in the Gospel of Mark.

2. Lüdemann, *Paul*, 10 (the sub-title of the book is *Founder of Christianity*).

3. Lüdemann, *Paul*, 10.

4. Pervo (*Dating Acts*) suggests a date of c. 115 CE or, more broadly, 110–120 CE. My own judgment, however, is that Acts might not have been written until around the middle of the second century—in other words, almost a full century after the lifetime of Paul.

5. Pervo, *Dating Acts*, 51–147.

6. For example, the second-century *Acts of Paul and Thecla*.

7. It is occasionally suggested that 2 Cor 12:1–7 is a reference to this experience, but this is far from certain. The New Testament book of Acts describes the "something"—often referred to as Paul's "Damascus Road Experience"—in rather vivid detail, not just once but three times (Acts 9:1–19; 22:4–16; 26:9–18; some of the details differ from one account to another). Here as elsewhere, however, information in Acts must be accepted only with great caution (see pp. 105–7).

8. See, for example, 1 Cor 9:1–2; 2 Cor 11:5–6; 12:11–12; and Gal 1:1.

9. For examples of differing views of Paul in the early Church, see Meeks and Fitzgerald, *The Writings of St. Paul*, 169–351.

10. For example, George Bernard Shaw declared that "there has really never been a more monstrous imposition perpetrated than the imposition of the limitations of Paul's soul upon the soul of Jesus" (quoted in Meeks and Fitzgerald, *The Writings of St. Paul*, 418).

11. For examples, see Meeks and Fitzgerald, *The Writings of St. Paul*, 395–433.

Introduction

1. See, for example, Bultmann's initial essay on the subject, first circulated in German during World War II but later made available in English translation: "New Testament and Mythology"; see also Bultmann, *Jesus Christ and Mythology*.

2. Morris, *Epistles to the Apostle*.

3. See chapter 4 in this volume.

4. It is possible that a small fragment of it has been preserved in what we know as 2 Cor 6:14–7:1.

5. Pauline authorship of Philippians is occasionally questioned, and the great nineteenth-century German scholar Ferdinand Christian Baur (1792–1860) attributed only Romans, 1 and 2 Corinthians, and Galatians to Paul.

6. Ehrman, *Forged.*

7. Keck, *Paul and His Letters*, 17.

8. See note 6.

9. 1:1–2:13; 2:14–7:16 minus 6:14–7:1; 8:1–24; 9:1–15; 10:1–13:14; and 6:14–7:1.

10. 4:10–20; 1:1–3:1; and 3:2–4:9 (21–23) or, alternatively, 1:1–3:1 and 3:2–4:23.

11. Fee, *The First Epistle to the Corinthians*, 780–92.

12. Walker, *Interpolations*, 91–189.

13. Walker, *Paul and His Legacy*, 37–63, 95–122, 123–30, 181–99.

14. Walker, *Interpolations*, 190–236.

15. O'Neill, *Paul's Letter to the Romans* and *The Recovery of Paul's Letter to the Galatians.*

16. For a fuller discussion of interpolations, see chapter 9 in this volume.

Paul on the Historical Jesus

1. Bultmann, *Theology of the New Testament*, 1:188.

2. Gal 2:7 also refers to Peter. Most scholars assume that Peter and Cephas are the same. My own judgment, however, is that Gal 2:7b–8 is a later, non-Pauline interpolation; see my *Paul and His Legacy*, 37–63.

3. For example, in his discussion of what Christians should or should not eat (1 Corinthians 8, 10:14–33; Romans 14), Paul might have appealed to the saying attributed to Jesus in Matt 15:10–11 and Mark 7:14–15.

4. See chapter 2 in this volume.

5. Dunn, *The Theology of Paul the Apostle*, 184.

6. Dunn, *The Theology of Paul the Apostle*, 184.

7. Borg, *Reading the Bible Again for the First Time*, 242.

8. See also Mark 7:15: "There is nothing outside a person that by going in can defile, but the things that come out are what defile."

9. See chapter 3 in this volume for a discussion of whether "faith in Jesus Christ," "put our faith in Christ Jesus," and "faith in Christ" are the correct translations of the Greek. The point, however, is that "no one will be justified by works of law."

10. Borg, *Reading the Bible Again for the First Time*, 254; see also Scroggs, *Paul for a New Day*, 10.

11. Sheldon, *In His Steps.*

Chapter 2

Paul on Repentance and Forgiveness

1. *Aphesis* also appears twice in Luke 4:18, but the meaning is "release" or "liberation," not "forgiveness."

2. Matt 6:12 (twice), 14 (twice), 15 (twice); 9:2, 5, 6; 12:31 (twice), 32 (twice); Mark 2:5, 7, 9, 10; 3:28; 4:12; 11:25; Luke 5:20, 21, 23, 24; 7:47 (twice), 48, 49; 11:4 (twice); 12:10 (twice); 23:34.

3. As indicated in the Introduction, most scholars regard 2 Timothy, along with 1 Timothy and Titus, as pseudonymous (that is, written not by Paul but rather by a later *Paulinist* who claimed the apostle's name and authority to address a new set of issues).

4. See Walker, *Interpolations*, 166–89, for the argument that Rom 1:18–2:29 is a later, non-Pauline interpolation (most scholars, however, regard this material as authentically Pauline).

5. See the discussion of pseudonymity in the Introduction.

6. Dunn, *The Theology of Paul the Apostle*, 323–33.

7. An additional six times in the disputed letters.

8. An additional two times in the disputed letters.

9. An additional three times in the disputed letters

10. An additional five times in the disputed letters.

11. 1 Thess 2:16 (which is probably part of a later interpolation); 1 Cor 6:18; 7:28, 36; 8:12; 15:3 (which is apparently part of a pre-Pauline tradition); 15:17, 34; 2 Cor 5:19; 11:7; Gal 1:4; 6:1; Rom 2:12 (which may be part of a later interpolation); 3:23, 25; 4:7–8 (a quotation from Ps 32:1–2); 4:25; 5:12, 14, 15, 16, 17, 18; 6:15; 11:11, 12, 27 (apparently a paraphrase of Isa 59:20–21); 14:23.

12. See especially Rom 5:12–21; 6:6–23; 7:5–8:10.

13. In the undisputed letters, "Satan" appears only seven times (1 Thess 2:18; 1 Cor 5:5; 7:5; 2 Cor 2:11; 11:14; 12:7; and Rom 16:20). In the disputed letters, "Satan" appears at 2 Thess 2:9 and 1 Tim 1:10; 5:15. "The Devil" never appears in the undisputed letters, but it does occur eight times in the disputed letters (Eph 4:26; 6:11; 1 Tim 3:6, 7, 11; 2 Tim 2:26; 3:3; and Titus 2:3).

14. See Rom 7:7–13.

15. Gaventa, *From Darkness to Light*, 44.

16. For more on this, see chapter 3.

Chapter 3

Paul on Justification

1. Slightly revised version of William O. Walker, Jr., "Did Martin Luther Get It All Wrong about Faith in Christ?" *The Fourth R* 29,6 (Nov–Dec 2016) 7–9, 18. Copyright © 2016 Polebridge Press. Reprinted with permission.

2. The New American Bible, the official Roman Catholic translation, is very close to the New Revised Standard Version here; it reads (emphasis mine): " (yet) who know that a person is not justified by works of the law but through *faith in Jesus Christ,* even *we have believed in Christ Jesus* that we may be justified by *faith in Christ* and not by works of the law, because by works of the law no one will be justified."

3. See Gal 2:15–21; 3:1–14, 23–29; 5:2–6; Rom 3:21–31; 4:1–25; Phil 3:9.

4. The phrase actually appears in five different forms: *pistis Iēsou Christou* (Rom 3:22; Gal 3:22), *pistis Iēsou* (Rom 3:26), *pistis Christou Iēsou* (Gal 2:16), *pistis Christou* (Gal 2:16; Phil 3:9), and *pistis tou huiou tou Theou* (Gal 2:20; the last three words mean "of [or "in"] the Son of God"). For the sake of consistency and simplicity, however, I shall use *pistis Christou* in the discussion that follows.

5. A good summary of the debate can be found in Part II (pp. 33–92) of Johnson and Hay, *Pauline Theology*, vol. 4.

6. See, for example, 1 Thess 1:7; Gal 3:22; Rom 1:16; 3:22; 4:11; 10:4.

7. For example, Rom 1:8, 12; 3:3; 4:5. The article is absent, however, in Rom 4:16, where the genitive is clearly a *subjective* genitive.

8. English translations—including the King James Version—regularly translated *pistis Christou* as "Christ's faith" until the Revised Version in 1881 adopted "faith in Christ."

9. Some years ago, I asked the then chair of Trinity University's Department of Classical Studies how he would translate *pistis Christou*; his immediate response was "Christ's faith" or "Christ's faithfulness."

10. Indeed, Rom 4:16 has the phrase *ek pisteōs Abraam*, which exactly parallels *ek pisteōs Iēsou (Christou)* in Rom 3:26 and Gal 3:22.

11. See also Rom 1:8, 12; 1 Cor 2:5; 15:14, 17; 2 Cor 10:15; Phil 2:17; 1 Thess 1:8; 3:2, 5, 6, 7, 10; Philemon 5, 6.

12. *Hypakoē pisteōs* should be translated as "the obedience (*hypakoē*) that is faith/faithfulness (*pistis*)." The same phrase appears at Rom 16:26, but this is widely regarded as part of a later addition (interpolation) to the letter.

13. See the entire passage Rom 5:12–21.

Chapter 4
Paul on Eschatology

1. See especially Mark 13, Matthew 24, and Luke 21. There is considerably less eschatological material in the Gospel of John.

2. Despite some disagreement regarding whether 2 Corinthians represents a combination of parts of two or more originally separate letters, scholars are in general agreement that this section was composed *later* than 1 Thessalonians and 1 Corinthians.

3. I should note that I myself regard 1 Cor 15:29–34 as a later, non-Pauline interpolation; see Walker, *Paul and His Legacy*, 95–122. Even so, verse 32 might represent a more-or-less accurate reflection of something that actually occurred in Ephesus. Most scholars, however, do not see 15:29–34 as an interpolation.

4. Because of its relatively late date (early-to-mid-second century in my judgment) and theological agenda (including a "domestication" of Paul), Acts should be used only with great caution as a historical source. Nevertheless, Acts 19:23–41 may reflect an actual event in the life of Paul.

Chapter 5
Paul on Universal Salvation

1. Boring, "The Language of Universal Salvation in Paul," 275.

2. Essentially the same idea is expressed in Romans 2, which can be summarized by the following words in verses 6–8: "For [God] will repay according to each one's deeds; to those who by patiently doing good seek for glory and honor and immortality, he will give eternal life; while for those who are self-seeking and obey not the truth but wickedness, there will be wrath and fury" (verses 6–8). Romans 2 may, however, be part of a later, non-Pauline interpolation, and, if so, it should not be viewed as an expression of Paul's thought (see Walker, *Interpolations*, 166–89).

3. Boring, "The Language of Universal Salvation in Paul," 276–77.

4. Boring, "The Language of Universal Salvation in Paul," 277–88.

Chapter 6

Paul on Women

1. Slightly revised version of William O. Walker, Jr., "Paul on the Status and Role of Women: The Apostle as Radical Egalitarian," *The Fourth R* 25,2 (March–April 2012) 5–9, 22. Copyright © 2012 Polebridge Press. Reprinted with permission.

2. First Cor 11:3–16; 14:34–35; Col 3:18–19; Eph 5:22–33; 1 Tim 2:9–15; 5:11–15; 2 Tim 3:6–7; and Titus 2:3–5. In addition, see 1 Pet 3:1–7, which is not attributed to Paul but is the only other passage in the entire New Testament advocating male dominance and female subordination (it is in this passage that the often-quoted characterization of woman as "the weaker sex" appears).

3. George Bernard Shaw, "Preface" to *Androcles and the Lion* (quoted in Meeks and Fitzgerald, *The Writings of St. Paul*, 417).

4. The Revised Standard Version translates the Greek word in Rom 16:1 as "deaconess," but the New Revised Standard Version correctly renders it as "deacon" (the form is the same as that used when the term is applied to males).

5. To be sure, 1 Timothy is attributed to Paul, but, as will be noted later, most scholars regard it as pseudonymous. See also the Introduction in this volume.

6. I have argued elsewhere (Walker, *Paul and His Legacy*, 65–87) that the words "there is no longer male and female" are likely to be Paul's own addition to the baptismal formula.

7. See also Col 3:11 (probably pseudonymous): "there is no longer Greek and Jew, circumcised and uncircumcised, barbarian, Scythian, slave and free; but Christ is all and in all."

8. Walker, *Paul and His Legacy*, 265–86, especially 278–81.

9. See the discussion of pseudonymity in the Introduction to this volume.

10. For New Testament examples of household codes or passages that contain some features of such codes, see Col 3:18–4:1; Eph 5:21–6:9; 1 Tim 2:1–2, 8–15; 5:1–8; 6:1–2; Titus 2:1–10; 3:1–2; and 1 Pet 2:13–3:12.

11. The Stoic philosopher Seneca (4 BCE–65 CE), for example, refers to "that department of philosophy which … advises how a husband should conduct himself towards his wife, or how a father should bring up his children, or how a master should rule his slaves" (Seneca, *Ad Lucilium epistulae morales*, 11).

12. See chapter 9 is this volume and, for a detailed discussion, Walker, *Interpolations*.

13. See, for example, Fee, *The First Epistle to the Corinthians*, 780–92. See also the discussion of the passage in chapter 9 of this volume.

14. Walker, *Interpolations*, 91–126.

15. See Brooten, *Women Leaders in the Ancient Synagogue*.

16. Luke 8:2–3; 10:38–42; Mark 15:40–16:8/Matt 27:55–28:10/Luke 23:49–24:11.

17. Luke 14:26; Matt 10:34–37/Luke 12:51–53; Mark 3:31–35/Matt 12:46–50/Luke 8:19–21; Mark 10:29–30/Matt 19:29/Luke 18:29–30; Mark 13:12/Matt 10:21/Luke 21:16.

18. But see Walker, *Paul and His Legacy*, 65–87, for the view that Paul himself may have added "there is not male and female" to the pre-Pauline baptismal formula.

Chapter 7

Paul on Sex

1. Slightly revised version of William O. Walker, Jr., "Maybe Paul Didn't Hate Sex: A Response to Stephen Patterson," *The Fourth R* 27,5 (September–October 2014) 11–14. Copyright © 2014 Polebridge Press. Reprinted with permission.

2. Patterson, "Saint Paul Hated Sex."

3. *Porneia* is typically translated as "fornication" or "impurity," but it can refer to any type of illicit or forbidden sexual activity, including especially prostitution or sexual relations with a prostitute; see 1 Cor 5; 6:13, 18; 7:2; 2 Cor 12:21; Gal 5:19. For the related verb *porneuein* ("to fornicate"), see 1 Cor 6:18; 10:8; for the related noun *pornē* ("prostitute"), see 1 Cor 6:15; for the related noun *pornos* ("fornicator"), see 1 Cor 5:9, 10, 11; 6:9.

4. Most of Patterson's article deals not with what Paul has to say about sex *per se* but rather with the two passages in which he appears to address what today would be called "homosexual" activity (1 Cor 6:9 and Rom 1:26–27). I am in agreement with most of what Patterson says about these two passages; see my "What the New Testament Says about Homosexuality," reprinted in slightly revised version as chapter 8 in this volume. As Patterson points out, an assessment of Paul's attitude toward homosexual activity depends in part upon the translation and interpretation of the Greek words *malakoi* and *arsenokoitai* in 1 Cor 6:9 (see Patterson, "Saint Paul Hated Sex," 13). It also depends, however, in part upon whether Rom 1:26–27 was written by Paul (see my discussion of these verses later in this chapter).

5. My translation here and elsewhere in this chapter.

6. The Greek phrase translated as "a sister-wife" is *adelphēn gynaika* (accusative singular of *adelphē gynē*) and is sometimes rendered "a sister (that is, a believer) as wife." It is true that *gynē* can mean simply "woman," but most commentators agree that it here means "wife." Thus, the phrase *adelphē gynē* would mean "a wife who is a believer."

7. For the argument that Rom 1:18–2:29 is a non-Pauline interpolation, see Walker, *Interpolations,* 166–89. For a general discussion of interpolations in the Pauline letters, see Walker, *Interpolations*, and, for an abbreviated treatment, see Walker, "Interpolations in the Letters of Paul" (reprinted in slightly revised version as chapter 9 in this volume).

8. It is not the "unnatural" sexual activity, however, that is the basic sin; rather, such activity is viewed as the result of, or even as God's *punishment* for, the more basic sin of *idolatry* (Rom 1:24, 26, 28: "God handed them over").

9. Commentators have for the most part ignored the fact that the Greek word here is "person" (*anthrōpos*), not "man" (*anēr*), as would be expected in association with "woman" (*gynē*). I have no explanation for this, but it is noteworthy.

Chapter 8

Paul on Homosexuality

1. Slightly revised version of William O. Walker, Jr., "What the New Testament Says about Homosexuality," *The Fourth R* 21,3 (May–June 2008) 9–12, 26. Copyright © 2008 Polebridge Press. Reprinted with permission.

2. Furnish, *The Moral Teaching of Paul*, 65.

3. As noted in the Introduction in this volume, although 1 Timothy is attributed to Paul, it is widely regarded as pseudonymous. Some have argued that Mark 10:6–9 and Jude 6–7 should be added to the list, but most scholars agree that these passages have nothing to do with homosexuality.

4. In the New Testament, see, for example, Matt 15:19; Mark 7:21–22; Luke 18:11; Rom 1:29–31; 13:13; 1 Cor 5:10–11; 2 Cor 12:20–21; Gal 5:19–21; Eph 4:31; 5:3–5; Col 3:5–9; 1 Tim 6:4–5; 2 Tim 2:3–4; Titus 1:7; 3:3; 1 Pet 2:1; 4:3, 15; Rev 9:21; 21:8; 22:15.

5. In much of what follows, I am indebted to Martin, *Sex and the Single Savior*, 37–50.

6. Martin, *Sex and the Single Savior*, 39.

7. Martin, *Sex and the Single Savior*, 43.

8. Martin, *Sex and the Single Savior*, 38–43. To be sure, inclusion of *arsenokoitai* in a list of vices suggests that the root meaning has a negative connotation, but the basis for such a connotation may be more complicated than it appears.

9. For discussion, see, e.g., Furnish, *The Moral Teaching of Paul*, 67–72; see also 58–67 and the entire chapter, 52–82.

10. American Psychological Association, "Answers to Your Questions About Sexual Orientation and Homosexuality."

11. Martin, *Sex and the Single Savior*, 57.

12. I myself regard Rom 1:26–27 as part of an interpolation (later non-Pauline addition), but this is a minority view (see Walker, *Interpolations*, 166–89).

13. Furnish, *The Moral Teaching of Paul*, 78.

Chapter 9

Interpolations in the Letters of Paul

1. Slightly revised version of William O. Walker, Jr., "Interpolations in the Letters of Paul," *The Fourth R* 23,4 (July–August 2010) 15, 18–22, 24. Copyright © 2010 Polebridge Press. Reprinted with permission.

2. For a full discussion of interpolations in Paul's letters, see Walker, *Interpolations*.

3. The Emperor Constantine instructed Eusebius to prepare fifty copies of the Bible in Greek (around 331 CE). This may have been an attempt to standardize the text, and other such attempts may well have been made earlier.

4. Critical scholars generally agree that the pseudo-Pauline letters are 1 and 2 Timothy, Titus, Ephesians, Colossians, and 2 Thessalonians.

5. The same Greek word is used for "greater" in 12:31a and for "greatest" in 13:13.

Chapter 10

Paul and Other New Testament Authors

1. As noted in the Introduction, however, six of these—1 Timothy, 2 Timothy, Titus, Ephesians, Colossians, and 2 Thessalonians—are likely pseudonymous (that is, written by someone other than Paul but attributed to him).

2. In addition, although it does not mention Paul by name, 1 Peter appears to have been heavily influenced by Paul and/or his letters and is sometimes referred to—along with 1 and 2 Timothy, Titus, Ephesians, Colossians, and 2 Thessalonians—as one of the *Paulinist* writings. Some scholars have also found Pauline influence both in the Gospel of Mark and particularly in the Gospel of Luke.

3. The portrayal of Paul in Acts also differs from those in the various pseudo-Pauline writings, but I shall not examine these differences, confining my remarks to what appears in the authentically Pauline letters.

4. First Cor 9:1–2; 2 Cor 11:5; 12:11–12; Gal 1:1. See also Rom 1:1; 11:13; 1 Cor 1:1; 2 Cor 1:1; 11:5–12:12.

5. To be sure, the title "apostle" is applied to Paul twice (both in the same passage: 14:4, 14), but it is applied only in passing, and it is *plural*, including both Paul and Barnabas.

6. Gal 1:11–12; see also 1 Cor 9:1.

7. This dependence is strongly implied by the report that he was baptized by Ananias, spent "some days" with "the disciples" in Damascus following his "conversion" and baptism (Acts 9:10–25), and then went to Jerusalem, where he spent time with the believers there (Acts 9:26–30).

8. Gal 1:15–24. Note the assertion in verse 20: "In what I am writing to you, before God, I do not lie!" This suggests that Paul is here on the defensive.

9. Note that there is no reference to Arabia.

10. The visit three years after his "conversion" (Gal 1:18–24), a second visit for the "Jerusalem Conference" (Gal 2:1–10), and a projected third visit to deliver an "offering" to the Judean Christians (1 Cor 16:1–4; Rom 15:25–32). Second Corinthians 8 and 2 Corinthians 9 also speak of an offering for the believers in Judea, but they say nothing about *Paul* being the one to take this offering to Jerusalem.

11. He was "brought up" in Jerusalem at the feet of Gamaliel (Acts 22:3) and was present at the stoning of Stephen (Acts 7:58; 8:1).

12. The visit during which he was introduced to the apostles and preached in Jerusalem (Acts 9:26–30); the visit in which he brought relief in time of famine (11:27–30; 12:25); the visit for the Jerusalem Conference (15:1–29); a visit to greet the church (18:22); and the final visit when he was placed under arrest (21:17–23:31).

13. Acts 23:16–22.

14. For example, he appears to accept a subordinate role in Gal 2:2; just a few verses later, however, in Gal 2:6, he appears to disregard entirely the supposed authority of the Jerusalem leadership.

15. This is particularly evident in Acts 15:1–29 (the account of the Jerusalem Conference) and in Acts 21:18–26, where Paul accepts the advice of James and "the elders" that he follow a Jewish rite of purification.

16. For a discussion of this phrase, see chapter 3.

17. Acts 13:38–39.

18. Acts 15:8–11.

19. See especially Gal 2:11–14, where Paul rebukes Cephas in Antioch (but note also Gal 1:6–9; 2:4–10; 3:1–5; 5:7–12; 6:12–13; 1 Cor 1:10–17; and 2 Cor 10–12, where he rails against "super-apostles" who oppose him and his gospel.

20. Gal 2:7–9.

21. Acts 15:7. See also Acts 10:1–11:18.

22. Assuming that it is pseudonymous, proposed dates range from c. 80 CE until mid-second century.

23. It is addressed in more of them if the letters widely regarded as pseudo-Pauline (1 Timothy, 2 Timothy, Titus, Ephesians, Colossians, and 2 Thessalonians) are viewed as authentically Pauline.

24. If Paul's letters were at the time regarded as scripture, this might explain, at least in part, why the author feels it necessary to refer to them.

25. It would appear that "our beloved brother" is simply the author's way of maintaining a fictional identity as "Peter" (see 2 Pet 1:1, 13–14, 16–18; 3:1), who, of course, did know Paul. The phrase might also, of course, be an example of verbal irony (that is, saying the exact opposite of what is really meant).

26. Scholars who favor authenticity and an early date sometimes argue that Paul knew and was responding to James. Those who favor pseudonymity and a late date are inclined to maintain that James knew and was responding to Paul, Paul's letters, and/or Pauline Christians.

27. Gen 15:6, however, is in no way related to Abraham offering Isaac on the altar; rather, it relates to Abraham's response to God's promise of numerous off-spring.

28. There are other indications that the author of James may have known Paul's letters. For example, the following words appear both in Paul's letters and in James but nowhere else in the New Testament: *parabatēs* ("transgressor" or "violator"; Rom 2:25, 27; Gal 2:18; Jas 2:9, 11); *akroatēs* ("hearer"; Rom 2:13; Jas 1:22, 23, 25); and *katakauchaomai* ("to boast"; Rom 11:18 [twice]; Jas 2:13; 3:14).

29. The Greek word here is *telos*, which can mean "end," "goal," "purpose," etc. The entire verse is problematic, but my own translation is, "For Christ is the end of the law as a means of justification for everyone who has faith."

Epilogue

1. Walker, *Interpolations*.

2. Walker, *Paul and His Legacy*.

3. To be sure, some of these conclusions are based on my conviction that certain passages in the Pauline letters are later interpolations.

4. Bruce, *Paul, Apostle of the Heart Set Free*.

Bibliography

American Psychological Association. "Answers to Your Questions about Sexual Orientation and Homosexuality." Washington: The American Psychological Association, 1998.

Bartsch, Hans-Werner, ed. *Kerygma and Myth: A Theological Debate.* 2 vols. London: S.P.C.K., 1953–62.

Borg, Marcus J. *Reading the Bible Again for the First Time: Taking the Bible Seriously But Not Literally.* San Francisco: HarperSanFrancisco, 2001.

Boring, M. Eugene. "The Language of Universal Salvation in Paul." *Journal of Biblical Literature* 105,2 (1986) 269–92.

Brooten, Bernadette J. *Women Leaders in the Ancient Synagogue: Inscriptional Evidence and Background Issues.* Brown Judaic Studies 36. Chico, CA: Scholars Press, 1982.

Bruce, F. F. *Paul, Apostle of the Heart Set Free.* Grand Rapids: William B. Eerdmans Publishing Company, 1977.

Bultmann, Rudolf. *Jesus Christ and Mythology.* New York: Charles Scribner's Sons, 1958.

_____. "New Testament and Mythology: The Mythological Element in the Message of the New Testament and the Problem of its Re-interpretation." Pp. 1–44 in *Kerygma and Myth.* Vol. 1. Ed. Hans-Werner Bartsch. London: S.P.C.K., 1953.

_____. *Theology of the New Testament.* Vol. 1. New York: Charles Scribner's Sons, 1951.

Dunn, James D. G. *The Theology of Paul the Apostle.* Grand Rapids: William B. Eerdmans Publishing Company, 1998.

Ehrman, Bart D. *Forged: Writing in the Name of God—Why the Bible's Authors Are Not Who We Think They Are.* New York: HarperCollins Publishers, 2011.

Epp, Eldon Jay. *Junia: The First Woman Apostle.* Minneapolis: Fortress Press, 2005.

Fee, Gordon D. *The First Epistle to the Corinthians.* Rev. ed. The New International Commentary on the New Testament. Grand Rapids and Cambridge: William B. Eerdmans Publishing Company, 2014.

Furnish, Victor Paul. *The Moral Teaching of Paul: Selected Issues.* 2d ed. Nashville: Abingdon Press, 1985.

Gaventa, Beverly R. *From Darkness to Light: Aspects of Conversion in the New Testament*. Overtures to Biblical Theology 20. Philadelphia: Fortress Press, 1986.

Johnson, E. Elizabeth, and David M. Hay, eds. *Pauline Theology*. Vol. 4, *Looking Back, Pressing On*. Society of Biblical Literature Symposium Series 4. Atlanta: Scholars Press, 1997.

Keck, Leander C. *Paul and His Letters*. 2d ed. Proclamation Commentaries. Philadelphia: Fortress Press, 1988.

Lüdemann, Gerd. *Paul: Founder of Christianity*. Amherst, NY: Prometheus Books, 2002.

Martin, Dale B. *Sex and the Single Savior: Gender and Sexuality in Biblical Interpretation*. Louisville and London: Westminster John Knox Press, 2006.

Meeks, Wayne A., and John T. Fitzgerald, eds. *The Writings of St. Paul: Annotated Texts, Reception and Criticism*. A Norton Critical Edition. 2d ed. New York and London: W. W. Norton & Company, 2007.

Morris, Colin M. *Epistles to the Apostle: Tarsus—Please Forward*. London: Hodder and Stoughton, 1974.

O'Neill, J. C. *Paul's Letter to the Romans*. Baltimore: Penguin Books, 1975.

_____. *The Recovery of Paul's Letter to the Galatians*. London: S.P.C.K., 1972.

Patterson, Stephen J. "Saint Paul Hated Sex." *The Fourth R* 26,6 (November–December 2013) 13, 16.

Pervo, Richard I. *Dating Acts: Between the Evangelists and the Apologists*. Santa Rosa, CA: Polebridge Press, 2006.

Scroggs, Robin. *Paul for a New Day*. Philadelphia: Fortress Press, 1977.

Seneca, Lucius Annaeus. *Ad Lucillium epistulae morales/Epistulai morales ad Lucillium*: English & Latin. Trans. Richard M. Grummere. Vol. 3. Loeb Classical Library 214. Cambridge, MA: Harvard University Press, 1925.

Sheldon, Charles M. *In His Steps: What Would Jesus Do?* New York: Grosset & Dunlap, 1935.

Tyson, Joseph B. *Marcion and Luke-Acts: A Defining Struggle*. Columbia, SC: University of South Carolina Press, 2006.

Walker, William O., Jr. "Did Martin Luther Get It All Wrong about Faith in Christ?" *The Fourth R* 29,6 (November–December 2016) 7–9, 18.

_____. "Interpolations in the Letters of Paul." *The Fourth R* 23,4 (July–August 2010) 15, 18–22, 24.

_____. *Interpolations in the Pauline Letters*. Journal for the Study of the New Testament Supplement Series 213. London and New York: Sheffield Academic Press (A Continuum Imprint), 2001.

_____. "Maybe Paul Didn't Hate Sex: A Response to Stephen Patterson." *The Fourth R* 27,5 (September–October 2014) 11–14.

_____. *Paul and His Legacy: Collected Essays*. Salem, OR: Polebridge Press, 2015.

_____. "Paul on the Status and Role of Women: The Apostle as Radical Egalitarian." *The Fourth R* 25,2 (March–April 2012) 5–9, 22.

_____. "What the New Testament Says about Homosexuality." *The Fourth R* 21,3 (May–June 2008) 9–12, 26.

Index of Modern Authors
and Editors

About the Author

William O. Walker, Jr. (Ph.D., Duke University) is Jennie Farris Railey King Professor Emeritus of Religion at Trinity University in San Antonio, Texas, where he served as a member of the faculty and as an administrator from 1962 until his retirement in 2002. The author of *Gospels, Jesus, and Christian Origins* (2016), *Paul and His Legacy* (2015), and *Interpolations in the Pauline Letters* (2001), he has served as co-author, editor, associate editor, or assistant editor of a number of other books, including *The HarperCollins Bible Dictionary* (1996), and has published more than seventy articles on New Testament topics. He is a member of *Studiorum Novi Testamenti Societas,* the Society of Biblical Literature, the Catholic Biblical Association of America, and is a Fellow of Westar Institute.

CPSIA information can be obtained
at www.ICGtesting.com
Printed in the USA
BVHW041740030220
571300BV00015B/261